W O R S H I P ♥ M A T T E R S

Central
Things

Worship in Word and Sacrament

Gordon W. Lathrop

D1167104

Augsburg Fortress

CENTRAL THINGS
Worship in Word and Sacrament

Editors: Suzanne Burke, Jessica Hillstrom
Cover and interior design: Laurie Ingram
Cover photos: Bible, photo © Brand X Pictures/PunchStock; baptismal font,
Prince of Peace Lutheran Church, Burnsville, MN, © Augsburg Fortress; cup
and bread, photo by Marty Berglin, © Augsburg Fortress

ISBN 0-8066-5163-6

Manufactured in the U.S.A.

Julie Mastell

Contents

Preface

The present book considers what worship in word and sacrament actually is and why it matters so much. In Christian worship, there are certain central things that we hold and, even more, that *hold us* into hope and faith and life.

These reflections are, in the first place, a considerably rewritten second edition of the essay that appeared as "What are the essentials of Christian worship?" in the first volume of the series *Open Questions in Worship*, published by Augsburg Fortress in 1994. I am deeply grateful to Samuel Torvend, who welcomed and cared for the first version of this essay, and to Suzanne Burke, Robert Buckley Farlee, and Martin Seltz for the invitation to contribute such a rewritten edition to the Worship Matters series. The issues and topics being considered in that series and the leadership of these editors matter greatly to all of us.

Other parts of this volume were first delivered as a lecture given at both the Lutheran Theological Seminary in Hong Kong and the Lutheran Institute for Theological Education in Bangkok, Thailand. I thank Mabel Wu, Jukka Helle, and the faculty and students of these schools for their hospitality to me and their discussion of these ideas.

Scriptural quotations within the text of this volume are drawn from the New Revised Standard Version of the Bible. Quotations from the Lutheran Confessions are taken from Robert Kolb and Timothy Wengert, eds., *The Book of Concord* (Minneapolis: Fortress, 2000). The translation of the significant sixty-seventh chapter of the *First Apology* of Justin Martyr is my own, having first appeared in my *Holy Things* (Minneapolis: Fortress, 1993) and *Holy Ground* (Minneapolis: Fortress, 2003).

In 1959, in an important little book entitled *Worship in Word and Sacrament* (St. Louis: Concordia, 1959), Lutheran theologian Ernest B. Koenker, wrote, "Together, worship, Word, and Sacrament embody the living Christ, whom we encounter in the service; when and where this occurs, tired, harassed people experience the joy, the renewal, the edification, that comes only from the life of God" (pp. 7–8). Half a century later, this assertion is still true and, if anything, even more urgent.

Gordon W. Lathrop

1
What Are the Essentials
of Christian Worship?

The things that happen in public worship matter. Let us begin with that assertion.

But what things? That is to say, what exactly do we *do* if we mean to enact Christian worship? This question is critical for us if we care about the clarity of the Christian faith in our time. The ways the Christian faith is acted out, symbolized, spoken, and publicly *done* when we gather together as a church matter immensely to anybody who wonders whether Christianity has anything to offer today to people who search for meaning. More, Lutheran Christians argue that the things we do in the Christian assembly should primarily be the things that make it possible to believe in God at all. Hospitality therefore requires that our worship services should be clear about the sources of meaning among us, about the basis for our hope, the nature of our faith. The apostle Paul urged just such hospitality, just such clarity in the worship of the early Christian congregation in Corinth (see 1 Cor. 14:14-16). But perhaps this clarity concerns not only the visitor or the seeker. Perhaps most of us are among those who wonder what Christianity really means in the present time. Perhaps most of us come to church hoping to find something that will help us to believe in God again today. What will that something be?

We may ask the questions in even greater urgency and greater detail: What things do we really need to have for this to be a Christian gathering? What words should we speak or sing? What patterns should we follow? What marks public worship as authentically Christian? Perhaps most important, to what God do the matters at the heart of our worship actually bear witness?

Of course, most of us do not usually ask such questions. When we engage in Christian worship, when we go to church, we do what this congregation or parish to which we belong "has always done." Well, not quite always. We know that. Rather, we do this current Sunday's particular version of a pattern of Christian worship received by this congregation. In many churches the pattern is printed in books, replete with directions for action and words for speaking and singing. In other churches the pattern is just as apparent, though not written: the song of the musical group or the sermon of the pastor, say, is always expected to take a certain place in the order of unfolding events. In both cases, the recurring and expected elements of the service are the predominant characteristics we sense in worship. They always connect to our memory of other times we have gone to church. They help us know that this is *church*. Then certain changing elements—the scripture readings for today, the names of the sick in the prayer this week, the particular name of one who is being baptized now—are gathered into that seemingly timeless pattern. Indeed, the repetition of patterned actions and words into which present details may be inserted means that Christians, too, do "rituals," to call our practices by the name anthropologists would use were they studying us. Christians call these rituals by the name "liturgy." Whatever our Christian assembly does when it gets together, whatever pattern of communal action we follow, written or unwritten, that is our *liturgy*. Thus, no churches are "nonliturgical" churches. The only question is *what* liturgy, what pattern of communal action, we follow when we get together.

But these rituals or liturgies, these patterns of actions and words that constitute worship, have developed differently in different Christian communions. Indeed, sometimes the most important value such rituals seem to communicate may be familiarity: by this or that characteristic, we know we *belong*, we know it is *our group* doing the ritual. The central matters in any congregation may have become these markers of familiarity. Then, one way or another, the question with which we began returns. Here are some of the forms of that question: What is it that makes it possible to be in a gathering that is not our own and recognize it as Christian? Do our markers of familiarity communicate anything important about the Christian God?

More: even Christians who belong to the same denomination or the same congregation may experience great differences in the ceremonies they conduct. Some argue that the Sunday gathering should be filled with new things. Others argue that it should be marked by traditional things. What ought to hold them together? Indeed, as these Christians seek to encourage each other toward a renewal of faith and practice in the present time, what exactly should they renew? What do we actually mean when we talk about "renewing worship"?

Furthermore, as Christianity finds itself in diverse cultural situations throughout the world, it seeks to find ways to let the historic faith come to expression in the words, music, gestures, and worldview of those cultures. In regards to Christian worship, what exactly should be so "inculturated"?

In addition, in present North American life, many Christians discover that their neighbors have practically no memory of Christian worship, that they are coming fresh to Christian faith when they come to church. To what essentials in Christian worship should they be introduced?

Interest in ecumenism, concern for congregational unity, work for denominational renewal, for global mission, for inculturation, and for evangelization can all bring along this question, in one form or another: What exactly do we do if we mean to enact Christian public worship?

Are there any shared Christian *central things*?

Again, we may answer this question for ourselves by simply pointing to the practice of our own church. We do what our books or our current directives or our leaders say. We use our denomination's printed liturgy book or a pattern for worship that our pastor or one of our musical groups discovered somewhere. Or we use our own congregation's time-honored though unwritten order for a worship meeting. We find renewal by following this authority. Such a disciplined practice, cherished as it may be, does not set us free from the question, however. For example, in the quest for Christian unity, we cannot simply insist on our discipline for other churches. In the quest for renewal, we cannot avoid asking *what* is to be renewed. The liturgy in our congregation may make use of a book or the pastor's chosen pattern, but *we* enact it, *we* do it. When we do so, certain matters will take center stage, will seem to be what our meeting is most truly about. Do those matters genuinely express the heart of the Christian faith? Do the matters at the heart of our actual services belong among the essentials of Christian worship?

We might refuse this question altogether. Some people see Christianity as a fundamentally plural phenomenon, diverse from its very beginning, and they see any attempt to find the "essentially Christian" anything—including worship—to be, at best, a doomed undertaking and, at worst, an act of ideological tyranny. From this point of view, there are no "essentials of Christian worship." There are only the diverse ways Christians actually worship. There are only local communities holding concrete and quite diverse worship services. These diversities may be described, personally chosen, or ignored, but they cannot be united.

People who care about Christian worship need to listen to this point of view. There can be a kind of promotion of "essentials" which pushes legitimate diversity aside, sometimes doing so for the sake of an unexamined desire for power or an illegitimate desire for uniformity. These concerns do not nullify the primitive Christian interest in "unity in Christ" nor the New Testament assertion of the "one baptism" (Eph. 4:5) and of the "one body" that partakes of the "one bread" (1 Cor. 10:17; cf. 12:13). It is still possible to inquire about the essentials while welcoming a full diversity of local worship practice. After all, embracing diversity also holds the potential of refusing to face the urgent question of unity, choosing rather to cleave only to that which belongs to me and to my group.

But other Christians have recently refused the question in another way. Arguing that there are no central Christian worship actions, they assert that what is essential to Christian worship is a particular evangelical Christian notion, even a Christian slogan: "God's gracious plan for the purpose of your life" or "Jesus as your personal savior," for example. Christian worship may do anything—most especially, it may do anything that is accessible and effective for the "unchurched," anything seen as meeting their needs—as long as it carries and communicates this idea. Liturgies with this idea at their heart are sometimes called "seeker services."

Again, those who care about the health of Christian worship should pay attention to the passion for the gospel and for the "outsider" in this proposal. Healthy Christian worship must always share that passion. But communal actions are not just neutral, capable of bearing any idea. If a Christian worship service is, say, much like television entertainment in its format and style, one must seriously question whether any idea of God's grace, which might indeed be mentioned in the talk of the leader or in the song of the musical group, will be communicated. Or, if a congregation sets out to church-shoppers a "menu" of "worship opportunities," distinguished on the basis of style preference, one must seriously question whether anything other than style and choice will finally come across. In such cases, we have to wonder whether any idea will be heard as strongly as will the values of the entertainment industry: the values of celebrity, of a marketing response to human needs, and of our ability to choose between the things the show is offering us.

In any case, Christian faith is more than an idea and more than the centrality of our own choice. Say it this way: *Christian worship is the communal encounter with the grace of God incarnate in Jesus Christ, and it involves the encounter with those concrete, flesh-and-blood things that connect us to the flesh of Jesus and so engage us in that grace.* If that is true, then whatever it is that unites a Christian assembly—whatever is offered to a newcomer, is shared in Christian mission, is renewed in a renewal movement—must have something to do with these things. Welcoming others must involve welcoming them to a real community and to communal action focused around these very things. The central symbolic actions that Christians do must surely be set out in accessible, hospitable love, but they cannot be dispensed with.

Then what are those symbolic actions? We are back to the question.

Many Christians in our day dare to answer this question in increasing convergence with each other. One of the most significant statements on Christian unity in recent years, the World Council of Churches document *Baptism, Eucharist and Ministry*, makes clear by its title two of the central matters of worship: the water-bath we call "baptism" and the meal we call by many names. According to the same document, the ministry, the leadership of the church, is able to carry out its chief responsibility "to assemble and build up the body of Christ" principally "by proclaiming and teaching the word of God, by celebrating the sacraments, and by guiding the life of the community" (Ministry, 13 [Geneva: World Council of Churches, 1982], p. 22).

In fact, many Christians use the phrase "word and sacrament"—a phrase familiar and dear to Lutherans—as shorthand for what they believe are the essentials of the Christian assembly. Thus the United

Methodist Church calls its basic Sunday service "A Service of Word and Table" (*Book of Worship*, 1992, 33–80). The basic movement of the Presbyterian "Service for the Lord's Day" includes "the Word" and "the Eucharist" (*Book of Common Worship*, 1993, 46). The Roman Catholic Church makes a parallel assertion in what many consider to be the key passage of the *Constitution on the Sacred Liturgy*, the first document to come from the Second Vatican Council (on December 4, 1963) and one of the most important results of the movement for liturgical renewal in the earlier twentieth century. The document states that Christ is present in the church in the *sacraments*, especially baptism and eucharist, in his *word*— "since it is he himself who speaks when the holy scriptures are read in the church"—and *in the gathering of the church*, "for he promised: 'Where two or three are gathered together in my name, there am I in the midst of them'" (*Constitution on the Sacred Liturgy*, 7 [Collegeville: Liturgical Press, 1963], pp. 7–9).

Indeed, many of us, in many denominations, find a new clarity of "word and sacrament" in our churches. That is, we find something of these things: a new accent on the importance of scripture reading in harmony with other Christians using a common lectionary, a shared collection of appointed readings; a new sense of the importance that preaching and hymn singing should arise out of and support these texts we have read; a new sense of the importance of celebrating baptisms in the midst of the community as it is gathered; a new vigor in the intercessions of the community; and a continued growth in the frequency of the celebration or reception of the Lord's supper.

We, too, may join this ecumenical company of Christians and assert that there are indeed essentials in Christian worship. These essentials are, quite simply, a community gathered around word and sacrament. Worship that carries this Christian center, holds these things as central, is "worship in word and sacrament." Or, to say the matter more fully, the essentials for Christian worship are *an open and participating community gathered on the Lord's Day in song and prayer around the scriptures read and preached, around the baptismal washing, enacted or remembered, around the holy supper, and around the sending to a needy world.*

Lutherans have found authority for such an assertion in their central and classic confession concerning the church, presented in Augsburg in 1530:

> It is also taught that at all times there must be and remain one holy, Christian church. It is the assembly of all believers among whom the gospel is purely preached and the holy sacraments are administered according to the gospel.

> For this is enough for the true unity of the Christian church that there the gospel is preached harmoniously according to a pure understanding and the sacraments are administered in conformity with the divine Word. It is not necessary for the true unity of the Christian church that uniform ceremonies, instituted by human beings, be observed everywhere. As Paul says in Ephesians 4[:4-5]: "There is one body and one Spirit, just as you were called to the one hope of your calling, one Lord, one faith, one baptism." (*Augsburg Confession*, 7, in Kolb and Wengert, *The Book of Concord*, p. 42)

Much more recently, an international gathering of Lutherans and other Christians, meeting in Cartigny, Switzerland, and struggling to think well about the lively relationship of worship and the many cultures of the world, said something quite similar:

> An examination of the tradition, from the Biblical witness, the early Church, and the Lutheran Reformation, reveals the core of Christian worship to be Word, Baptism, and Eucharist. The pattern, or ordo, of entry into the community is teaching and baptismal bath. The pattern of the weekly gathering of

the community on the Lord's Day is the celebration centered around the Word and eucharistic meal. These core elements are clearly evident in the historical witnesses of the Christian worship tradition. Further, it is evident that the purpose of this pattern of worship is faithfully to receive and faithfully to proclaim the Gospel of Jesus Christ. (Cartigny Statement on Worship and Culture, 3.7, in S. A. Stauffer, ed., *Worship and Culture in Dialogue* [Geneva: Lutheran World Federation, 1994], pp. 133–134)

The Evangelical Lutheran Church in America echoed the Cartigny Statement in its own assertion of 1997 in *The Use of the Means of Grace*:

We are united in one common center: Jesus Christ proclaimed in Word and sacraments amidst participating assemblies of singing, serving, and praying people. (Application 4b, *Principles for Worship* [Minneapolis: Augsburg Fortress, 2002], p. 100)

Even though we may join these voices, it remains for us to ask what "worship in word and sacrament" actually means. That is, first of all, why is it actually these things that are essential to Christian worship? Do we find any deeper meaning in their centrality than the sheer assertion that it is so? Second, what actually are these things? What is essential to doing them? And third: What would it actually mean for our worshiping communities to regard the Cartigny "core" as the core also for us? What would happen if the central things were, in fact, truly central in our gatherings? We will take up this second and third complex of questions in the second half of this book, in chapters four through seven. But first we should think more carefully about the reasons for *word and sacrament in a participating assembly* comprising the essentials of Christian worship. To those reasons we turn next, in the following two chapters.

_____

For reflection and discussion

1. What are the most important things your congregation does when it worships? Is it clear from the way they are done that they are important?

2. What do these things say about God?

3. Have you ever attended a Christian worship service where you felt strange, and where you perhaps wondered whether the service was in fact Christian? Why?

4. What are the "markers of familiarity" in your own congregation's worship? Would those markers be strange to someone else, not a frequent participant in your assembly? Are they too central?

5. If a person who never visited Christian worship turned to you for help about what is going on in the service, what would you most like to explain?

6. What do you judge as the worst worship service you ever attended? Why was it so distressing?

7. One person remembers that, as a small child, he used to play church by singing the bids of the Kyrie and passing out bread, saying repeatedly, "Grace Lutheran Church! Grace Lutheran Church!" Another person remembers playing at candle-lighting and taking the offering. If the children of your congregation had seen worship only as your assembly does it, how would they play church? What would they do? Would they play the central things?

2
The Fruit and the Leaves
of the Tree of Life

At the end of the Revelation to John, the writer of the book speaks of seeing the holy city of God "coming down out of heaven." Then he describes that city:

> I saw no temple in the city, for its temple is the Lord God the Almighty and the Lamb. And the city has no need of sun or moon to shine on it, for the glory of God is its light, and its lamp is the Lamb. The nations will walk by its light, and the kings of the earth will bring their glory into it. Its gates will never be shut by day—and there will be no night there. People will bring into it the glory and honor of the nations. But nothing unclean will enter it. . . . Then the angel showed me the river of the water of life, bright as crystal, flowing from the throne of God and of the Lamb through the middle of the streets of the city. On either side of the river is the tree of life with its twelve kinds of fruit, producing its fruit each month; and the leaves of the tree are for the healing of the nations. (Rev. 21:22-27a; 22:1-2)

Of course, according to Christian faith, this vision is part of God's promise of the reconciling end for all things, of the time when the tears of all the peoples will be wiped away (21:4). In the text, the city is "coming down" now. Christians believe that what belongs to the end is also now coming to be present among us, wherever the Spirit of God poured out from the death and resurrection of Jesus Christ is present. According to the vision, at the last will be a great holy city, the "city of God." But a foretaste of that city, a witness to the God of that city, a beginning of the wiping away of tears, is present now wherever the church gathers.

Using this imagery of the Revelation to John, we can say that any gathering of the church should show some of the characteristics of the city. The presence of God and the Lamb—and the presence of the water of life and the tree of life that come from God—should be at the center of the assembly of the church. This assembly should be marked by the healing and grace-filled mercy of God's living presence, and not by sacrifices given as if to a distant or capricious god: "I saw no temple in the city" (21:22), no place of sacrifice. And the assembly should have open doors for all people to come in. These should be universal characteristics of the assembly called "church."

The text points to an openness to local reality as well. In the vision, the cultural gifts of the nations of the world ("the glory and honor of the nations") are to be given a critical and healing welcome into that city of God: "nothing unclean may enter there," but also "the leaves of the tree are for the healing of the nations." If the assembly of the church bears witness to that coming city, then that assembly ought also be open—critically, but still wholly open—to the cultural gifts of the people of all nations.

Christians have believed that when they read and sing and preach the scriptures in the heart of their gathering, God is there, speaking. Furthermore, Christians have believed that Jesus Christ—the Lamb—is truly present, giving himself away, and the Holy Spirit is truly poured out, making all things new, when they celebrate the holy supper or when they baptize a new member of the assembly. God and the Lamb are the light in the heart of the city through the word and the sacraments. Indeed, Christians have believed that baptism itself is immersion in the very river of the water of life and that to eat of the holy communion is to eat from the tree of life. These images of the magnificent, life-giving tree and the all-refreshing river are, of course, used in the Revelation as metaphors for the presence and grace of God in Jesus Christ. Word and sacraments apply that grace to human lives like the healing leaves, the reviving water, the life-giving fruit. Then Christians are becoming more and more aware that the door to this assembly around these gifts must be open to all people and that treasured cultural patterns from the nations should be welcome there.

We can take this text from the Revelation as a charter for the central things of Christian worship, the things that unite Christian assemblies and, at the same time, enable their diversities. Here are the themes for us: Recognize that every Christian assembly, everywhere, is to be a witness and sign of that one city. Celebrate word and sacraments as the principal and life-giving center of every assembly, especially every Sunday. Work on making sure that the door into every assembly is wide open. Understand that the assembly, its water and words and food, are being used by God now to begin to wipe away the tears from the faces of all peoples; they matter. Then, ask how the assembly may do its central work of word and sacrament and open door in ways appropriate to the gifts and dignity of each local place.

Such a charter is found, in different words and images, in the basic Lutheran confessional document, the Augsburg Confession. In its seventh article, which we have considered already (see p. 14), Lutherans have confessed that the church is always an assembly participating in God's gift of word and sacrament. Such is the universal character of the church. Then, as this gathering around baptism and word and supper takes place, the various other rites and ceremonies used by the gathering do not have to be everywhere the same. We will rightly have beautifully different ceremonial practices. But local rites and ceremonies do need to support the assembly gathering around the gospel of God in word and sacrament. To use the imagery of Revelation, they do need to "come into the city," by the light of God and the Lamb.

The Lutheran tradition of liturgy, at its best, is the tradition of this confession. A Lutheran approach to the Christian assembly for worship should always ask whether word and sacrament are strongly at the center of the meeting, graciously unobscured, speaking and doing the gospel of Jesus in clarity. Yet the worship service ought not look culturally and ceremonially the same in every place. The worship service ought to look like the city with its open gates. A Lutheran approach should ask if the door is open. Lutherans rightly ask these questions of themselves and they sometimes dare to take up the same themes in mutual affirmation and admonition of sister and brother Christians. For Lutherans, the true goal is not that all Christian assemblies be Lutheran, but that they all be gathered around the leaves and the fruit of the tree of life.

Taught by the classic approach of the Augsburg Confession, one North American Danish Lutheran congregation—in Luck, Wisconsin, in the nineteenth century—expressed what its worship was like by putting an inscription on its church bell. When the bell rang, inviting people to church, this congregation hoped that people would know that this is what the bell was saying:

> To the bath and the table,
> to the prayer and the word,
> I call every seeking soul.

When "every seeking soul" came through that open door, they could discover the presence of God and the Lamb, the water of life and the healing tree—the presence of the wiping away of tears itself—in that bath and table, prayer and word.

The inscription itself remained a little mysterious as to why seekers should come to the assembly and its central things. They would find out when they got there. "Come and see," said the disciples to each other as they began to gather around Jesus in the account of the Gospel of John (1:46). "Come and see," said Jesus himself to the disciples (1:39). Then the passage from the Revelation helps us to understand even more profoundly. *The central things of Christian worship are not so much things that we do as events where God has promised to act.* There is no "temple" in the city. God and the Lamb take its place. That is, our praise, our worship, our action, our sacrifice, even our seeking, are not the heart of Christian worship. God's presence, God's gift, the very fruit of the tree of life, is. Bath, table, prayer, and word are important to "every seeking soul" because God is there, wiping away tears, giving life.

The word *worship* can thus mislead us. The word can sound as if the praise we give to God is the heart of the matter, as if we call this event a *service* because we are giving service to God. The service, rather, is first of all a service God renders to any and all who come. Everything is turned on its head. It is not just "worship." It is "worship in word and sacrament," worship with the giving away of the leaves and the fruit of the tree of life at its center. In astonishing mercy, God uses our assembly, our words, our actions with water, bread and wine, our place and our time, as the means of the presence of these leaves and this fruit.

The other great mystery and mercy of the Luck bell inscription is found in the phrase, "every seeking soul." Actually, nobody else is invited. Only seeking souls. Yet, everybody is invited because that is what we all are. By this conception, if a service is worship in word and sacrament, then it is God's own "seeker-service."

Such worship, regardless of its diversities of expression, takes a simple and flowing shape. Faithful liturgy is more than our desire to praise God. It is more than a text. It is more than talk about the idea of God or the notion of the gospel. It is the flow of a communal action that is full of the overflowing grace of God, present in gestures and concrete signs as well as in words. Liturgy is word next to sacrament, prayers next to bath and table, water of life next to the fruit and leaves of the tree. This shape is implied by the Augsburg Confession. It rings out with the Luck bell. This shape is a useful tool for any church. This shape can be done everywhere, using local gifts, welcoming local cultures, encountering God's gift amid our actions.

In fact, such a shape can be traced to the earliest clear descriptions of Christian worship. As we will see, the second century account of Christian Sunday worship, written by the layman called Justin Martyr, describes an event that moves from gathering as a remembrance of baptism, to scripture reading, preaching and intercessions, then to giving thanks at table, communion, and the sending of help to the poor and sick (see pp. 79–80). Indeed, this pattern is the very one that is implied for the communities that originally read Luke's gospel. It is found in the report of the Sunday preaching and the "breaking of bread" both at Emmaus, in Luke 24, and at Troas, in Acts 20. It is found in the shape of the canonical gospel books themselves. Gathering, word, meal, and sending, by the understanding of Luke's gospel, are what we do on Sunday because they are the means of our encounter with the presence of the crucified, risen Christ, and the source of the mission we have from him in the midst of our current cities.

The *Use of the Means of Grace* puts the shape of Sunday worship in this way:

> We gather in song and prayer, confessing our need of God. We read the Scriptures and hear them preached. We profess our faith and pray for the world, sealing our prayers with a sign of peace. We gather an offering for the poor and for the mission of the Church. We set our table with bread and wine, give thanks and praise to God, proclaiming Jesus Christ, and eat and drink.

We hear the blessing of God and are sent out in mission to the world. (Application 34b, *Principles for Worship*, p. 124)

But then the same document makes clear who acts amid our actions:

Through this Word . . . as through the sacraments, God gives faith, forgiveness of sins, and new life. (Principle 5, p. 101)

At the table of our Lord Jesus Christ, God nourishes faith, forgives sin, and calls us to be witnesses to the Gospel. (Principle 31, p. 122)

Such a "shape" and such an application of the shape to doing liturgy in every local place are not only found in the earliest sources and in Lutheran texts. This shape is also important to current ecumenical discussion. Recent proposals from the Faith and Order movement use this shape to urge the renewal of the simple, universal Christian liturgy in each local place. The American Presbyterian *Book of Common Worship* talks about the Sunday service as following this outline: Gathering, Word, Meal or Eucharist, and Sending. The Renewing Worship project of the Evangelical Lutheran Church in America also follows this outline. In doing so, they join Luke and Justin and the Augsburg Confession and the Luck bell in making available to congregations the strongest schema with which to understand and organize actual parish worship. Indeed, the ELCA has used this simple schema to encourage new versions of multiculturally diverse but deeply Lutheran worship, appropriate to the current North American context.

Of course, other ways could be used to phrase this outline. But if we take the Augsburg Confession seriously and if we think that church should bear witness to the city of Revelation 21 and 22, then we will need something like this outline for our worship services. The outline itself should be encouraging and liberating. God's gracious gifts can be the center of our gathering, mercifully and really present in each local place, uniting us all in the unity God gives, allowing for rich local diversity. Word and sacrament at the heart of an assembly on Sunday: this is worship that is local and universal, marked by the central things and by the open door.

It is important to say what this does not mean. North American Christians have very widely celebrated and have very widely exported a kind of Christian worship that originated in the revivals of the nineteenth century American frontier, a time and place of few churches but occasional and wildly attractive open-air meetings. Sometimes people propose that such worship should become the new universal Christian pattern. According to this pattern, an opening warm-up that works to move people's hearts is followed by the reading of a few practical scripture verses and a powerful message or sermon focused on changing individual lives. These elements all lead to a variety of ways that people can indicate their own personal decisions to so change. Warmed hearts and personal decisions are, of course, often—though not always—good things. But, in this pattern, they are made to be the central things, the essentials of Christian worship. No. Lutherans and other Christians must say it clearly: When the choice of the individual self is placed at the center of the Christian meeting, instead of the grace of God, we will be malformed. We will miss the very heart of the gift: God's decision for the world and for life, no matter what we individually decide. We will miss the city and the diverse multitudes, the perspective that opens toward many other communal points of view, instead of just my own particular self. We will lose the intercessions for all the needs of the world. We will easily miss or obscure God and the Lamb, the water and the tree of life, word and sacrament as the center of the meeting.

The city of God is coming down from heaven. The tears are beginning to be wiped away. The dwelling of God is among the peoples, and all the nations are welcome to God's abundant healing. Such is the faith that may come to expression through worship in word and sacrament celebrated in each local place.

But if we can find help in thinking about the central things from the images of one biblical text, is such help to be found more widely in the Bible? Are there biblical sources for worship in word and sacrament? In the next chapter we consider these questions.

_____

For reflection and discussion

1. In Revelation 21 the city of God has no temple. Why not? What things might the lack of a temple mean?

2. What might it mean that God is "wiping away tears" now? Does this wiping away of tears happen in the service?

3. What does the word *worship* mean for you? Is it different or the same as the meaning of "worship in word and sacrament"?

4. In Luke 24:13-35, what does the Gathering look like? The Word? The Meal? The Sending?

5. How does your congregation concretely enact the parts of the outline "Gathering, Word, Meal, Sending"?

6. Can you imagine or have you seen a congregation from another culture that comes together—enacts the Gathering—in a way different from your congregation and yet still Christian? What things do you recall or imagine?

3
The Bible
and the Central Things

The New Testament is full of the central things. By considering the ways that this is true, we may come yet closer to the reasons for the centrality of bath, word, prayer, and table in our assemblies.

To the extent that it is possible for us to ascertain, all the communities behind the New Testament writings treasured *baptism*. Paul's letters, for example, presume the use of it as the way one enters the church (cf., for example, Rom. 6:3-4; 1 Cor. 12:13; Gal. 3:27-28). The gospels begin with it, modeling a pattern in which the Christian communities also begin.

The *reading of scripture* as a liturgical practice is implied by passages in Luke, where the interpretation of scripture by the risen Lord is probably a model of the church's Sunday meeting (Luke 24:27, 32, 45; cf. 4:21). Such scripture reading is also implied by passages in Paul, where the apostle's own letters are to be read in the gathered assembly (1 Thess. 5:27; Col. 4:16), and by the letters to the churches and the opening of the scroll in the Revelation to John (2-3; 5:1-10).

Preaching—like the risen Lord's interpretation of scripture on the first day of the week—is everywhere assumed. Paul says, "We proclaim

Christ crucified" (1 Cor. 1:23). The risen Christ in Luke says "that repentance and forgiveness of sins is to be proclaimed in his name to all nations" (Luke 24:47).

Praying for the needs of the world, praying confidently for others in Jesus' name and in the power of the Spirit, is implied by calling the church a "royal priesthood" (1 Peter 2:9). The New Testament conception of the whole church as a "priesthood" implies that the church stands before God in prayer on behalf of others. Such praying is explicitly directed in the Pastoral Letters: "First of all, then, I urge that supplications, prayers, intercessions, and thanksgivings be made for everyone" (1 Tim. 2:1).

Furthermore, the Christian practice of the *supper of the Lord* is assumed by the "do this" of Luke (22:19) and Paul (1 Cor. 11:24-25) and by diverse reports elsewhere in the New Testament. For example, that the meal is held every Sunday is reported for the community at Troas (Acts 20:7) and suggested by the first-day model of the Emmaus story: On the first day of the week, the risen Lord is known in the blessing and sharing of the bread (Luke 24:30-31).

Certain passages in the New Testament even hold more than one of these central actions together. At the beginning of Acts, after the baptism of a great multitude of new believers, the community is "devoted . . . to the apostles' teaching and fellowship, to the breaking of bread and the prayers" (2:42). At Troas, the community gathers on Sunday for preaching and the meal (Acts 20:7-12), the same pattern that is found in the disciples' first-day meeting with the Risen One on the way to Emmaus (Luke 24:13-35). In Mark, Jesus uses together the cup and baptism, central matters that the community knows, as metaphors for the martyr's death (Mark 10:38-39; cf. Matt. 20:22-23; Luke 12:50). Paul depends upon the community having baptism and the meal as central events in order to make his exhortation based on the baptism of Israel in the Red Sea and the holy eating and drinking of the exodus journey (1 Cor. 10:1-22) and in order to propose that baptism and the meal unite Christians in one body and one Spirit (1 Cor. 12:13).

None of these passages give us great ritual detail about what the churches did when they gathered for worship. But this much is clear: in New Testament texts, the risen Christ bids the community to teach and to baptize (Matt. 28:19; cf. Mark 16:16). The crucified Risen One is known in the explanation of scripture and in the meal (Luke 24:30-32; cf. John 20:20; Rev. 5:6-7). The community is to pray in confidence, speaking in the name of the Risen One (John 14:13-14; Mark 11:24). And preaching is to be full of the powerful weakness of the cross of Christ (1 Cor. 1:17). These assertions of Christian faith underline the crucial significance of these central symbolic acts already among New Testament era communities.

These assertions also do more. They help us to see the deepest reason why the actions are essential: they have to do with Jesus Christ. In these things we encounter the full reality of who Jesus is and what he does, and who we are as one body in Christ. Some ancient Christian communities certainly did other things when they worshiped. But these things—baptism, preaching, intercessions, the supper, or "the bath and the table, the prayer and the word"—are central to Christians because they have been seen as intimately bound up with who Christ is.

We see this connection of Jesus with those things that become the church's central actions already in the gospel traditions of his life. According to the gospels, Jesus himself was *baptized* (Mark 1:9 and parallels). He himself came *preaching* (Mark 1:14 and parallels) and *praying* (Mark 1:35). One of the ways he was most well-known— even notorious—was by his constant *table fellowship* with sinners (cf. Matt. 11:19; Luke 7:34). By this perspective, the church's gatherings around these very things continue the actions of Jesus himself.

Even more, the very shape of the gospel books seems to reflect the importance of these central things to the earliest gatherings of the churches. Even with their own characteristic additions, all four of the gospels follow the pattern first found in Mark: the *baptism* of Jesus leads to the stories about his healing actions and his words—to the *word*—and then to the account of his death and resurrection, the meaning of which is told most clearly at *meals*, at the last supper and at other meals before and after his death. This gospel-book pattern, which we have come to accept as if it were conventional, probably echoes the central patterns of the Christian community in the ways they preserved and told the story of Jesus, the story of the one whom they saw at the heart of their meetings.

We then see the connection of Jesus Christ to the core actions of the church's worship in the ongoing tradition of faith that participation in these things is participation in him. To be part of the community of preaching, baptism, and the meal is to be gathered by the power of the Spirit into him, under the grace of the God who sent him. To be in these things is to be in the life of the Holy Trinity. Thus, in the New Testament, Jesus Christ is the meaning of the *scriptures* and the content of *preaching* (Luke 24:27; 1 Cor. 1:23; Rev. 5:5); speaking of him is speaking the "yes" to all of God's ancient scriptural promises (2 Cor. 1:20). To so speak is to speak in the Spirit (John 16:14). *Baptism* is being buried with Christ in order to be raised to newness of life with him (Rom. 6:4), and this resurrection occurs "by the glory of the Father." Such baptism is being immersed in the one Spirit into the one body (1 Cor. 12:13). *Prayers* are "in his name" and filled with the presence of the Spirit (Rom. 8:16, 23). Indeed, he teaches a prayer that continues to stand for him and to sum up the prayers of the church (Matt. 6:9-13; Luke 11:2-4). Jesus Christ hosts the *supper* and is himself the gift given for eating and drinking (Mark 14:23-24 and parallels; Rev. 3:20); to eat and drink with him is to be formed as his body (1 Cor. 10:17) and to stand with him as he blesses and gives thanks to God. So are we all made to drink of the one Spirit (1 Cor. 12:13).

The New Testament does not give us a constitution of the church nor a service book. It does give us Jesus Christ, seen and known amid ordinary things: water for washing, words for telling important stories and for prayer, a shared meal. Just as access to Christ would be difficult and skewed for us without the New Testament books, so also we need the concrete signs of water, communal words, and shared meal. Without them, when we speak of Jesus Christ we could easily be speaking more of ourselves and of our own projections than of the biblical, historic Christ. It is easy to take a holy figure—"Jesus"—and make that figure a screen on which we project our own ideas or needs. But with these living actions, we actually encounter the very self of Jesus breaking into our projected ideas: in the teaching, baptizing church, "I am with you always" (Matt. 28:20); the scriptures themselves "testify on my behalf" (John 5:39); in the meal, "this is my body" (Mark 14:22). These things are central to us, because Christ is central to us. These things are the concrete way of our encounter with his flesh, with him who is for us the revelation and the gift of God's grace, the source of the outpoured Spirit.

Several important consequences follow from this deepest reason for the central things of Christian worship. For one thing, it is clear that we urgently need this core, these central actions. Now, in early twenty-first century North America, many people are talking about Jesus Christ. That name is used for many religious ideas present in our current culture: for success programs and for self-realization plans, for a character in best-selling novels or movies, for politics of the left and, especially now, of the right, for "values," for condemnations of people of whom we do not approve, for ideas about the "soul" and about world-escape. Indeed, for some the name *Jesus* is a perfect synonym for popular American religion or, simply, for one's own self. More scholarly sorts assume that the only access to Jesus is through reconstructions of what he might actually have been like, what he might actually have said or done. Such reconstructions are prey to the same pressures of current politics and religion. Yet, Christians have believed that who Jesus is and what he does are most reliably encountered in word and sacrament, that is, in the scriptures read next to that bath and that meal that are full of Jesus' own Spirit and Jesus' own self-giving.

We then begin to see why these things are set out, according to the

Luck bell, mysteriously, for "every seeking soul." In Christ, according to Christian faith, we meet the God who wipes away tears, gives life to the dead, promises and says yes to the promises, and sets out the food of forgiveness and festival. We need Christ, the historic biblical Christ, and not simply our own projections and ideas of him.

Why *these* things, specifically? Why not something else? Why not some other book or some other religious rites? Conch-shell blowing or incense-burning or pilgrimages or ecstatic speech, for example? Nothing is wrong with such rites, per se. In fact, some Christians make use of such rites in their own communities, as accessory to the central things. Furthermore, many other books besides the Bible are both beautiful and profound. But the stories of Israel read aloud in the assembly next to the ancient books from the earliest church are found by the church as the way to encounter Jesus Christ. The washing that is baptism and the supper that is "eucharist" were already present in his life, as witnessed in the gospels. Indeed, scripture reading and interpretation, praying, washing for purity before God, and prayers at meals or the meal-as-prayer were deeply present in the lay religious and Jewish culture in which Jesus' ministry first occurred. According to the New Testament, he made a new use of them for the purposes of his own mission. Then, these things were received, down through the ages, as gifts from him, done at his command. We might speculate about other possibilities, but we actually have no other means. These are the ones that are historically present in the New Testament and are found nearly universally in the life of the church. These concrete, real things connect us to a concrete, real history of his body, the church.

These things also connect us to the concrete, real earth. Even though we may say that we have these things simply because they are what actually comes to us from the culture in which Jesus was born and from the church's history, Christian faith has believed that the universal availability of the stuff of these central symbols has been and is a gift from God. Water is everywhere. Humans need it simply to live. Baptism is in water, any water, local water, not some special or Near Eastern water. Understandable but strongly symbolic speech, used to convey the deepest human values or pray the longings of the human heart, is found in every culture. The oral witness to Jesus Christ can be made in that language. The Bible can be translated into it. Prayers can be made in it, speaking out the needs of all the earth. Festive meals are found universally. The Lord's supper is held with local bread and local wine—or, where these are simply not available or are far too expensive or too alien, with locally recognized staple food and festive drink—not with special, imported food. The things in which we encounter Jesus Christ, and in him God's overflowing grace for all, are accessible everywhere. They are signs of the goodness of God's earth, as well as signs for the deep unity God's mercy can establish between the good diversity of the many cultures of the world.

In these central things, important local human materials are turned to new purpose. Local waters, local food, local language, local prayers are all now turned to the new purpose of the gospel.

Furthermore, word, bath, and meal can be seen as gifts inclusive in another sense. Words can be both praise and lament, the recounting of both death and life. Both are used in the stories of Israel and of Jesus and both are welcome in the prayers, songs, and preaching of the church. A bath can wash and a bath can drown. Both happen in the one use of water in the church. The joyful, life-giving meal of the community has the death of Jesus at the center of its memory and the dreadful hunger of our neighbors and of the world as the focus of our mission. The central things of Christian worship are not narrowly religious things, nor are they concerned simply with happiness and success. They welcome us to the full truth about ourselves and the world: sorrow and hope, hunger and food, loneliness and community, sin and forgiveness, death and life. God in Christ comes amidst these things, full of mercy.

That these historic, central matters of Christian worship correspond to God's mercy can be seen in the simplest encounter with their forms. Words may be *heard*, coming from outside of ourselves, giving us a new story or reinserting us in an old story, whereby we may understand ourselves and our world anew. Water may be *poured* over us, somebody else thereby immersing us in the bath. Food may be *given* to us—and to lines and lines of other people—pressed into our hands, reached to our lips. These communal gifts, in their very form, show forth and enact the Christian faith that God's grace in Christ by the power of the Spirit is our new story, our bath, our life-giving meal, our access to the tree of life.

But why all of these things? Would not just one be enough? No. The gift is more abundant than that. A set of words alone could easily be twisted into a new law, a list of things we have to do in order to be acceptable to God, unless it is constantly clear that the content of the words is the same content that is washed over us in the bath and given to us to eat and drink in the supper. Drinking the cup in which Christ says, "My blood, for you," gives us a key to understand the scriptures. Indeed, all preachers should strive to see that their sermons say in words the same thing that the bath and the cup say in actions. In the church, words should be edible, like bread, and just as full of grace. Conversely, the bread of Christ may be seen as a "word," one of the strongest words we have to speak the truth about God, the world, and ourselves. This is why, in the history of the Christian liturgy, the essential matters are always juxtaposed to each other and are always made up of at least two juxtaposed elements: word *and* sacrament, readings *and* preaching, praising *and* beseeching, teaching *and* bathing, thanksgiving *and* receiving the food, bread *and* cup.

It then becomes clear that Christian communities and their leaders share a responsibility to let these things always be and be seen to be at the center of our gatherings. Again, the word *worship* itself may mislead us into thinking that when we gather we may do anything that seems appropriate to us as "worship," any sort of singing, any sort of "god-talk," any sort of pious exercise. Yet if our gathering is about the grace of God in Jesus Christ, we cannot do without word and sacraments. To pretend that Christian freedom includes freedom from these central things of Christ may be only to choose the bondage of our own opinions, our own religion, our own, unquestioned selves, masquerading as "God."

These essentials of Christian worship should not be seen as a burden. They are gifts, to be celebrated as gifts, renewed by love and invitation and teaching, not compulsion. Indeed, great diversity is possible in the ways in which an assembly reads scripture and interprets it, washes those joining the community, and holds a meal. Many other secondary characteristics—musical style, architectural or artistic arrangement, patterns of entrance and of leaving, leadership—may make one assembly observing the central things seem very different from another.

What then actually *are* these central things? What would we be doing if we were doing them? What would it actually mean for our worshiping communities to regard them as core for us? In the following chapters, we will think through each of these central actions in turn, finally turning to the style or manner in which we do them, asking if there may also be something "essential" to which we should attend there.

For reflection and discussion

1. In order to illustrate what is meant by *preaching*, the children's book *Sunday Morning* (see bibliography) uses a picture of the women running from the empty tomb of Jesus to tell others about his resurrection. Why? How is preaching like that image?

2. Besides the story of the last supper, what Bible stories might help us to understand the meaning of the holy communion? How?

3. Besides the great commission (Matt. 28), what Bible stories might help us to understand the meaning of baptism? How?

4. Can you think of any Bible stories that tell of praying for others? Is your congregation's practice of prayer like these passages?

5. The author says that the water and words, bread and wine of Christian worship are "signs of the goodness of God's earth." Is this true? How is it true?

4
Central Things:
The Word and the Prayers

Christian worship includes scripture reading and preaching. It also includes praying for others. Such reading and preaching and praying are essential.

The assertion about scripture may be most clearly seen as true in the Christian Sunday or festival assembly, where scripture reading and preaching take a central role in almost all Christian communities. At other times, Christian communities may gather for prayer, and the Bible may indeed be read. Some Christian communities have used the weekdays as occasions to simply read the Bible straight through, book by book. But one old custom was that this further reading of the Bible would recall for us last Sunday's readings or move us toward the readings for the coming Sunday. A verse or two from the Sunday readings might be read as a summary reminder. An additional biblical text that illuminates the Sunday readings might be used. Then hymns might be sung, echoing the Sunday readings, and silence might be kept for the Sunday readings to keep on speaking. In fact, ecumenical work continues on a lectionary for daily use that will propose readings through the week that will echo and anticipate the readings of the surrounding Sundays.

But at the Sunday assembly itself the scripture is read in fullness, at the very heart of the meeting that is at the very heart of Christian identity.

It is not just any book that is read. It is not even an especially dear "religious" book. It is the scripture of the Old and New Testaments. On Sunday, in the Christian assembly, we should hear readers read aloud from the book that is made up of the writings recognized in the history of the church as authoritative and as appointed for public reading. Indeed, the canon—the list of writings in the Bible—is none other than that old list of books that may be read in church. A bound Bible is a single volume containing the books on that list. Ease of use in church is what led to the books being bound together. The Bible is a book that belongs to the Christian Sunday assembly.

Why the Bible? Because Israel's stories set next to the stories from the earliest church make it possible for us to know the truth about the world's need and about God's grace in Jesus Christ. Because Jesus Christ is the living embodiment of all of God's scriptural promises. Because on the day of resurrection, which is what Sunday is, the crucified and risen Lord interprets to us in all the scriptures the things concerning himself (cf. Luke 24:27), and our hearts burn with life at this word. Because the Spirit of God poured out from the death and resurrection of Christ enlivens this word in our hearts. Because the scriptures read in such a way surprise us with grace and bring us to know that God has not dealt with us as we might have expected. Indeed, so important are these reasons for Bible-reading that without such reading in the Sunday assembly, one may rightly doubt whether it is a Christian assembly at all.

Of course, it is possible to imagine desert-island situations or the life of refugees in extreme need, without any book, including the Bible. The form of the scriptures in such a situation may be simply a remembered verse or two, a paraphrased story, a hymn-stanza.

Ordinarily, though, when we gather on Sunday, the scripture is read. It should be read with great dignity, as if the reader were reading to us from the Book of Life itself or from the very words that create and sustain all things.

Christians do disagree somewhat about the actual list of books that may be read. Roman Catholics include the ancient Jewish books that were only preserved in Greek, not Hebrew. Protestants, following the counsel of Jerome, a crusty old biblical scholar of the late fourth and early fifth century, do not. Episcopalians and some Lutherans hold a median position, encouraging the secondary reading of these books—the so-called Apocrypha, books like the Maccabees, Tobit, the Wisdom of Solomon, and Susannah—but discouraging their use for the formation of doctrine. Yet, this minor disagreement should not distract us from the profound and widespread agreement: the biblical books are read so that Christ may be encountered. Indeed, Jerome himself articulated the universal faith of the church: "We eat the flesh and drink the blood of the divine savior in the holy eucharist," said he, "but so do we in the reading of the scriptures."

It is then not as history, moral lessons, or beautiful poetry that the scriptures are first of all read. They are read so that the community may encounter the truth about God in Jesus Christ enlivened by the living Spirit. They are read like the passage from Isaiah that Jesus read in the synagogue at Nazareth when he added: "Today this scripture has been fulfilled in your hearing" (Luke 4:21).

In fact, like the reading of the scriptures in the synagogue, in the time of Jesus and in Jewish practice of the present day, the Sunday reading of the Bible in the Christian assembly is best made up of more than one reading. In the synagogue, the *torah*-portion (a reading drawn from the first five books of the Bible, read according to a fixed annual or triennial cycle of selection) is followed by the *haftarah* ("completion"), which is a reading drawn from the rest of the Hebrew scriptures and chosen in relationship to the theme of the *torah* reading. This set of readings is then followed by interpretation through preaching, as Jesus did in the synagogue at Nazareth (Luke 4:16-27).

Since the earliest times in the church, there has also been more than one reading set next to preaching. Justin, the lay Christian teacher of the second century church in Rome, whom we already mentioned, wrote the clearest full description of the Christian Sunday assembly in about A.D. 150. The first part of his description reads:

> And on the day named after the sun all, whether they live in the city or the countryside, are gathered together in unity. Then the records of the apostles or the writings of the prophets are read for as long as there is time. When the reader has concluded, the presider in a discourse admonishes and invites us into the pattern of these good things. Then we all stand together and offer prayer. (*1 Apology* 67; for the full text of Justin's account, see pp. 79–80)

Several things about this important description stand out. Christians meet on Sunday. One among their number presides, but other ministers include at least one reader. They hear a biblical sermon from the presider, who articulates the "good" or "beautiful" things of the readings. They pray together in intercession. Then, at the heart of this part of Justin's description, he notes that they hear several passages of scripture read aloud, from what we would call both the Old Testament and the New.

But it is not simply because of the historical precedent in Christian circles, nor because of the synagogue, the source for much Christian practice, that more than one reading is to be advised to Christians today, though these precedents should not be ignored. Rather, one passage, set next to another, set next to yet another helps us to see both the fullness of God's gift and the sense that it is not so much before the readings themselves as before the one whom they serve that we are gathered. Indeed, Christians understand all the readings in the assembly to be like the primary Christian metaphor for the four gospels: they are all, in their diversity, like the four great living creatures of Ezekiel (1:5ff.) and of Revelation (4:6ff.) who gather around the throne of God and of the Lamb. For Christians, in the midst of the readings stands the crucified, risen Christ, holding out his wounds for our life. For Christians, the Spirit of God, enlivening the words of the readings, draws us through reading and preaching and singing these words, into the life of the Trinity.

It is this understanding of the function of scripture in the assembly that led to the development of the lectionary used by many Christian churches. Although the use of such a collection of appointed readings is not an essential in Christian worship—as is the reading of scripture itself—a lectionary does help to make it clear that the churches gather *together* before the word of God, as before a *gift*, and not that the churches or the preachers choose scripture passages according to their own moods or their own agendas or their own projections. A lectionary does help us all—lay people and clergy alike—to know what readings we are going to read in the assembly this week.

The current ecumenical three-year lectionary, widely used with slight variations in Roman Catholic, Lutheran, Anglican, and Protestant churches, chooses a first reading from the Old Testament to relate to the theme of the third reading, drawn from one of the gospels, rather like the synagogue *haftarah* was chosen in relationship to the *torah*. A reading from the letters of the New Testament is placed second, representing the churches that live from these scriptures. The risen Christ encountered in the gospel reading, whom the assembly greets with acclamations like "Glory to you, O Lord!" is then seen to be alive and present in *all* the readings. Such a gift from the tradition of Christian worship should not be lightly set aside. Those Christian assemblies who choose another manner of ordering their public reading of scripture should ask whether their manner as profoundly represents the Christian understanding of scripture, as richly sets one text next to another around the living God and the Lamb. Those assemblies who do use this lectionary should also take time to understand its structure and intention. The lectionary is the congregation's book and needs to be more widely known.

In many churches these readings are surrounded by a pattern of song and action that makes the Christian use of the scriptures clear. Psalmody and hymnody place the biblical text in the mouth of the whole assembly, in forms appropriate to communal song. Indeed, the word of God is the whole church's business and God is rightly addressed as present in the readings. A psalm, often with a repeated refrain, is used to receive and to meditate on the first reading. All the readings may conclude with acclamation by the assembly, praising the triune God who is present now with such mercy and life-giving wisdom here. "Holy wisdom, holy word," the reader might call out at the end of each of the first two readings, calling our attention to the living presence of the Spirit in what has been read, in what echoes now in the room and in our ears and hearts. "Thanks be to God!" we respond. An alleluia verse usually greets the reading of the gospel, the risen Christ being greeted with the old Hebrew word that Christians have long used for the celebration of the resurrection. The community stands for this third reading, addressing its acclamations to the Risen One, not because it is the most important reading, but because the story of Jesus—with the crucified and risen Christ seen as present to us now in that story—is taken as the interpretive key to all the scriptures, like Jesus opening the ancient books to his disciples on the first Sunday (Luke 24:27).

But whether or not the lectionary is used, whether or not these ceremonies are used, the scriptures are read at the Sunday meeting.

At best, this reading will be one text set next to another and then yet another, followed by preaching. Preaching, too, is an essential of Christian worship. Or, rather, the complex of scripture readings set next to preaching makes up one of the central things. Preaching, in this sense, is not just any speech, not even an especially religious speech, certainly not just a recitation of the current theories or insights or experiences of the preacher. Preaching that belongs to the essentials of Christian worship is a freely composed address, juxtaposed to the appointed readings, that opens up the appointed readings to the assembly in such a way that their Christian intention is clear. The *Use of the Means of Grace* says:

> Preaching is the living and contemporary voice of one who
> interprets in all the Scriptures the things concerning Jesus Christ.
> In fidelity to the readings appointed for the day, the preacher
> proclaims our need of God's grace and freely offers that grace,
> equipping the community for mission and service in daily life.
> (Application 9a, *Principles for Worship*, p. 104)

And such preaching will articulate our utter need, our loss, failure, sin, and death, using especially the images of the day's texts to do so. It also articulates God's healing mercy in Christ. It will "preach Christ crucified" (1 Cor. 1:23) as present in the readings. It will begin to wipe away tears. It will invite us to see our own lives according to the pattern of the good things of the scriptures, as Justin said. It will speak with a voice that makes it possible for us to believe again: "So faith comes from what is heard, and what is heard comes through the word of Christ" (Rom. 10:17). It will say in living words what the bath and the meal say in actions.

Thus the "word" in the Christian assembly takes at least two forms: the classic written texts of scripture read aloud and the living voice of the preacher. These two forms are juxtaposed, even in a certain tension with each other. The texts always say more than the sermon can say, with an overflowing richness of meaning. Yet the sermon articulates the Christian purpose of reading the texts at all: that we, by the Spirit, may meet God's grace in Christ and trust it for our life. The sermon presses the texts to their function as the "living creatures" around the living God. When preaching does not play this role, an essential element in Christian Sunday or festival worship is missing and the assembly is much diminished.

To make clear that this assembly around scripture and preaching is an assembly before God, the gathering is marked by prayer and hymnody. The classic Western liturgy has come to celebrate the entrance into this service of readings and preaching with certain fixed songs—an entrance hymn or gathering song, the Kyrie litany and/ or the "Glory to God"—and with a traditional opening exchange of greetings, the apostolic greeting, and a traditional opening prayer, called now the "prayer of the day." These songs, this mutual greeting, and this prayer are remarkable gifts. They express the faith in the triune God and speak with intertwined praise and petition. They join us to a very large community that has used these texts as the way to gather. They enact a deep mutual regard between the assembly and its presider. And, with the new three-year set of prayers made available through the initiatives of the Renewing Worship project, they give us fresh words, related to the day's readings, with which to begin our gathering. But what is essential then is not so much these particular elaborations as the sense that whatever is done must serve to gather us before God and give centrality to the reading of scripture.

The central thing is reading and preaching, set side-by-side.

These two forms of the word—reading and preaching set next to each other and together making up that "word" that is essential—press us beyond, to something more. Lutherans have long responded to the reading and preaching of God's word with the communal singing of the most important hymn of the service, the "hymn of the day." It is as if the single voice of the preacher broadens to become the communal voice of the assembly, all of us, all together, taking up the responsibility of proclamation. Many Christians have further used this place in the service as the place in which the community responds to the word by its confession of faith in the words of one of the classic creeds.

Even more importantly, though, the reading and preaching together lead us to prayer, to intercession for all the needs of church and world, and they invite us to the holy supper. Naming God's promises in the texts and preaching the one who is the fulfillment of God's promises awaken us to speak before God the names of many people and situations in the world that seem to be without promise. Proclamation yields to intercession; the truth of God embraces the truth of our world. Such intercessions, crafted as the priestly work of the people of God for the sake of the world this day, led by one of the assembly and responded to by all, belong to the central things of Christian worship. A Christian gathering on Sunday should not fail to pray for the unity and mission of all the churches, for the well-being of the ecological systems and diverse species of life on the earth, for the nations and cities of the world, for our enemies, for people in need, for people outside of this assembly and strange to us, and for the sick and the dying.

Such intercessions should tell the truth. That is, they should be truly intercessions, naming real needs in expectation and hope before God. They should not be little sermons about ourselves or to ourselves, cast in prayer form. Nor should they only be about the needs in our congregation, though these needs may certainly make up a part of the prayers. Rather, the intercessions invite the entire assembly to be involved in prayer on behalf of the whole needy world. The intercessions are part of the open door of the liturgy, here an open door toward the agonies of the people and the creatures of all places. They will best be led by a lay assisting minister who has a heart for the world's needs and a gift for such leadership and who has trained that gift to help the entire assembly be attentive to simple prayer. The intercessions will reflect what is in the daily newspaper, but they will also be marked by things that do not make the news or things that no longer draw attention on the front pages: threatened species, polluted waters, and people who are afraid, alone, hungry, mourning, laid off from work, laboring for peace, hoping to adopt a child, and on and on. It is a moment for truth and genuine, hopeful prayer.

And it is a moment for hunger. For hearing this word, we are now invited to taste the one of whom we have heard, bearing these gifts away in mission. So we turn to the supper.

For reflection and discussion

1. Do you read the appointed readings for Sunday before you go to church, perhaps on Saturday or on Sunday morning? Does it make any difference in the way you participate in the service? What difference?

2. Have you ever been a reader in the Sunday service? What does it mean to you?

3. Do you know how your pastor prepares to preach? Could you help? How?

4. What makes for a good sermon?

5. Check what the prayer of the day is in your congregation for the coming Sunday. Then read the readings for that Sunday again, together with the text of that prayer. How do they go together?

6. Check what the hymn of day is in your congregation for the coming Sunday. Then read the readings for that Sunday and the text of the hymn. How do they go together?

7. Now, today, what are needs in the world for which a Christian community should pray? Make as long a list as you can.

8. Look around in your assembly's worship space, your congregation's sanctuary. Many churches use images of the four living creatures (human figure, lion, ox, and eagle; see Ezek. 1:5ff and Rev. 4:6ff) in one or more ways in their room. Does yours? What do you think these images mean in the place or places where you find them? What other symbols do you find? How do they relate to the central things?

5
Central Things:
The Table and the Sending

The meal, Christ's gift of himself in bread and cup, is essential in Christian worship. That table-participation gathers us into God's mission to the world.

This assertion ought also be seen as true in the principal Sunday and festival gatherings of all the communities of Christianity. In fact, for a variety of reasons, the meal has shrunk, no longer to be recognized as a meal in many places, eaten only by the leaders in others, having little to do with this world in many others, or disappearing altogether on many Sundays in others. Without having to assign blame or sort out the complicated histories of these developments, it is clear for us that such evidence as we may garner from the New Testament churches, from the early centuries of the church, and from the first years of the Reformation, indicates that from the very beginning Christians regarded every Lord's Day as the occasion for the Lord's supper. Thus, the community at Troas gathers for "the breaking of the bread" on the first day of the week (Acts 20:7). The first- or second-century community of the writing called the *Didache* is exhorted "on the Lord's Day of the Lord come together, break bread and hold Eucharist" (*Didache, 14:1,* in Kirsopp Lake, ed., *The Apostolic Fathers*, vol. 1 [Cambridge,

MA: Harvard, 1959], p. 331). The Lutheran churches of the early sixteenth century confess that "among us the Mass is celebrated every Lord's day and on other festivals" (*Apology of the Augsburg Confession, 24:1,* in Kolb and Wengert, *The Book of Concord,* p. 258).

[handwritten margin note: Why we share communion every Sunday]

But the recovery of full participation in the holy supper as the principal service of every Christian community on every Sunday remains our goal not simply because of historical or confessional wisdom, though these sources are not to be ignored. Rather, it is because we need it. We need the meal side-by-side with the scriptures in order to understand what the scriptures are about. We need to hear "This is my body" and "This is the new covenant in my blood" in order to encounter Jesus Christ in truth. We need to receive those repeated words "for you" and the gifts they accompany in order ourselves to believe and to live in the all-encompassing forgiveness they convey. We need to continually practice word next to meal, meal after word, in order for any newcomers—and the constant "newcomer" in us all—to see what Christianity itself is about, let alone what any Sunday is about: not just ideas and words, but the presence and mercy of Jesus Christ, the fruit and leaves of the tree of life. We need to eat together this simple meal, full of God's overflowing gift and yet, at the same time, only making us all hungrier for God's justice and mercy to flow throughout the whole world. We need to be continually formed into "one bread" with all the little, hungry ones of the world who belong to Christ. We need to keep, as the central symbol of our week, a shared meal of justice and love, where food is shared equally with all, where the goodness of God's earth is respected and consumed only within limits, and where food and help are also sent to those outside this circle.

The meal of Christ's gift is one of the essentials of Christian worship, especially on every Sunday and festival.

The *meal*? Is it really a meal, this broken bit of bread, this sip of wine? Yes. In fact, the supper of the Lord is made up of the old beginning of a Jewish meal (when God was blessed and thanked over a loaf of bread that was then shared as the inauguration of common eating) together with the old end of such a meal (when God was praised at length over a cup of wine that was then shared around the table to conclude the gathering). In the earliest Christian churches, this bread and cup still framed a full meal. Then, over the first century of Christian life, the food, which continued to be brought to the gathering of the church, or the money, which was brought in order to purchase food, came to be given away. This may be because persecution forced the common meal to be held in the morning rather than at supper time. Or it may be that Christians came to concur with Paul's criticism of the factions, favoritism, and power plays that could occur at such a "church supper" as inappropriate to the meal that proclaims Christ's death (1 Cor. 10–11). In any case, the resulting shape of the supper was a new kind of meal: one that could be eaten by many, many people at once; one wherein thanks were said over the bread and the wine together as the very signs filled with Christ's gift of himself; and one where much food and money were still brought but, except for the loaf and the cup, all of it was to be given away to the hungry.

Our mid-second-century writer, Justin, immediately after his description of the gathering for scripture reading, preaching, and prayer, continues to describe the Sunday gathering of Christians in Rome:

> When we have concluded the prayer, bread is set out to eat, together with wine and water. The presider likewise offers up prayer and thanksgiving, as much as he can, and the people sing out their assent saying the *amen*. There is a distribution of the things over which thanks have been said and each person participates, and these things are sent by the deacons to those who are not present. Those who are prosperous and who desire to do so, give what they wish, according to each one's choice, and the collection is deposited with the presider. He aids orphans and widows, those who are in want through disease or through another cause, those who are in prison, and foreigners who are

sojourning here. In short, the presider is a guardian to all those who are in need. We hold this meeting together on the day of the sun since it is the first day, on which day God, having transformed darkness and matter, made the world. On the same day Jesus Christ our savior rose from the dead . . . he appeared to his apostles and disciples and taught them these things which we have presented also to you for your consideration. (*1 Apology* 67; for the full text of Justin's description, see pp. 79–80)

Several further things should be noted about this important description. The meal was held every Sunday, immediately following the scripture reading, preaching, and prayers. The presider gave thanks—as well or as long as he or she could—but everyone participated in this thanksgiving, both by their audible *amen* and by their eating and drinking. The loaf and the cup of communion were sent to those who could not be with the assembly—whether because of sickness or imprisonment or their status as slaves is not clear—by the hands of table-servers or deacons. A collection was always made for the poor. Such a collection of food and money belongs essentially to the Christian meal and is one source of our continued practice of taking a collection on Sunday (cf. 1 Cor. 16:2).

So, this "meal" is a *meal* because it is a loaf to eat together and a cup to drink together, because it is accompanied by a meal prayer, because it longs for a feast for the poor, and because, in all of this, it tastes the very banquet of God's mercy.

Then, just as with the "word," the "table" of Christian worship practice is made up of two things together, pressing us toward a complex third. In the word, scripture reading is set next to preaching, and these two together bring us to intercession, inviting us to the meal. In the table, thanksgiving is set next to eating and drinking, and these two together press us toward collection for the hungry and toward mission in the world.

Food is set out. Not just any food, but a loaf of bread, which is widely seen as the principal staple food in human communities and which connects to Jesus' meals, and wine, which is widely seen as the principal festive drink in human communities and which also connects to Jesus' meals. In some places of the world, because of the scarcity of wheat bread and/or grape wine and because of the great need to show that this gift of Christ is always a local, contemporaneous gift, some other staple food or festive drink may need to be used. But in North America, *our* need will be to see that food can be treasured and not just wasted, to see that food can have deep symbolic significance, and to connect with the great biblical tradition. Our need will be to see that the food of the Lord's supper is really food, and that it connects with the story of Jesus and with our daily life. So, most communities will use bread and wine. We will need to let it be seen that the bread is really bread and that a full cup of wine is available for all.

And thanks are given. That is, a single leader—usually the person who is presiding in the liturgy, usually, in fact, the same person who brought the scripture readings to living voice in the preaching—proclaims the praise of God over the bread and cup, doing so with the full assent and the active participation of the whole assembly. We all, standing around the table, respond with ancient responses, sing out refrains and the song of the angels. We say *amen*. This thanksgiving verbally sets the whole community in Jesus Christ, by the power of the Spirit, before the face of God. It proclaims the promise of God and claims that promise, present to all the world in Jesus Christ. It celebrates that God created all things and invites all to taste that creation restored in Jesus Christ and in the work of the Spirit. It laments the deep pains and losses of the world. It is honest about death. Yet it trusts that this very food of Christ is a foretaste of the time when God will wipe away all tears. At the heart of the thanksgiving, the very words Christ speaks at the supper are proclaimed, inviting all to hear and see what the meal is for and who is the true host. Because of the centrality of this thanksgiving, the entire meal and indeed the entire word-meal service, is sometimes called *eucharist*, from the old

Greek-Christian word for thanksgiving to God through Christ in the unity of the Spirit.

Even the very best thanksgiving we may make together, however, will never be enough. We cannot say enough, praise enough, beg mercy enough. So, we always conclude the thanksgiving with the prayer that Jesus gave us, the Lord's Prayer. Gathered by the Spirit, we pray as if we are always beginners again, making simple prayers for bread and forgiveness and deliverance for all the world.

The thanksgiving prayer, in whatever form it takes, gives words to the eating and the drinking that follow. But in the eating and drinking we receive a gift greater than any prayer can proclaim: here, by the power of the Spirit and the word of promise, is the *very encounterable self* of Jesus Christ—his body—and the *very life* of Jesus poured out as the promised new covenant—his blood. All who are present who belong to that body are given to eat and drink, and the food of communion is sent to those who are absent. With Christ, then, there comes to all the nations, to all outsiders, to us, all the riches and treasures, all the glory and all the grace, all the life, all the judgment but also all the mercy and forgiveness of God.

Yet the world is still hungry. Judgment unrelieved by mercy seems to be everywhere. Death seems the most final lot. If nothing else, this service helps us to speak these truths. So we have taken a collection, to make a little dent in the sorrow, to help a few, to bear witness to Christ among the poor—something like Jeremiah purchasing a field in the face of an overwhelming invasion in order to show God's promise of life and hope (Jer. 32). We do this because of Christ, because the Crucified One has gathered all the sorrow into himself and held us into believing that God's promise is finally for all the world. This liturgy has itself been part of God's mission in the world, God's love for the world. We ourselves have been made again into what we eat: body of Christ for our neighbor. So we then leave, on mission to live out our hope amid the conditions of the world, to turn toward others beyond this circle, to (like Jeremiah) "buy the field" in the circumstances of our life, to act out some of the justice for which we have prayed, to share food as it is has been shared here, to honor the earth like the gifts of the earth have been welcomed respectfully here, and, especially, to turn toward our neighbor with the same love and solidarity that have been shown to us. "Go in peace. Serve the Lord," cries out one of the lay ministers assisting the assembly. Or, more recently, to make that service of the Lord more explicit and to recall, with Paul, the one challenge made by the first church council ever held (Gal. 2:10), the lay assisting minister says, "Go in peace. Remember the poor." "Thanks be to God," we say, and go.

Of course, there are disagreements among Christians about what the presence of the body and blood of Jesus really means, and some of these disagreements are serious. There are also disagreements about what to call the meal, about the exact food that should be used, about the form of the thanksgiving, about the manner of distribution, and about who precisely should eat and drink. This assertion that the meal is central and is to be held every Sunday is not meant to circumvent the serious discussion that still needs to be held among many Christians in the hope of finding sufficient common ground to enable the richer fellowship of their churches. Even so, these disagreements should not distract us from the centrality of this biblical gift nor from the urgent though neglected role the Lord's supper plays in most of our diverse traditions. Despite the disagreements, Christ gives us the supper *in common*.

These things, then, belong to the "table": thanksgiving and eating and drinking. Together these things set us in mission.

Word and table—that is the pattern of the Sunday and festival service of the Christian assembly. Or, we could say it more fully in this way: the pattern is scripture readings and preaching, leading to intercessions, followed by thanksgiving and eating and drinking, accompanied by a collection and sending us away. But must it be in this order? Could it be table followed by word or preaching followed by scriptures? Conceivably, though the logic of the ancient order is simple and clear, and it is difficult to see why one would choose to change it, except to somewhat dubiously demonstrate one's own independence. Indeed, when set in the midst of a needy world, the order can be seen to follow a pattern that ought not be changed. The words of scripture and preaching lead us to speaking words in prayer on behalf of our neighbor and all the world. They also awaken in us a hunger and thirst for the taste of God's goodness. But the supper sends us away to be the body of Christ to our neighbor, to be for our neighbor what we have received in the supper.

For reflection and discussion

1. In what senses do the holy communion, as it is celebrated in your assembly, really seem like a meal?

2. Where do the bread and the wine used in your congregation come from? Does the bread look like bread, the wine like a shared communal drink? Could you help to supply this food?

3. Read through one of the prayers of thanksgiving used at the eucharist in your congregation. What are its most striking phrases? Where do they come from? What do they mean?

4. Have you ever been an assisting minister helping to serve the communion in your assembly or helping to carry the communion to the sick or the absent? What has it meant to you to do this?

5. Does your congregation ever make a collection of food—or money to buy food—during the service? How does this act relate to the holy communion? For what purposes is the collection that is usually taken in your Sunday liturgy intended? Why? How does this action relate to the holy communion?

6. The last words in the Sunday service of the French Protestants, the Huguenots, used to be, "Go in peace. Remember the poor." Those words are a quotation from the Bible. Read Galatians 2:1-10. What might those words mean to you if they were the last words at your Sunday service?

7. If it is not already, how could you help the Lord's supper to become the principal service of every Sunday in your congregation?

6
Central Things:
The Bath and the Assembly

Christian worship includes that washing by which persons are added to the community of Christ. This bath and the assembly it constitutes are among the essential central things.

Indeed, baptism, as the bath is called by all Christians, belongs to every Sunday. The Sunday gathering of Christians may actually include such a baptism of a new Christian, at the same time giving all those gathered an occasion to be once again reimmersed in baptismal meaning themselves. Or, the Sunday assembly of Christians may include some act or acts of the remembrance of baptism: simply walking past the water pool on the way into the gathering; confession and forgiveness as a return to the water; the sign of the cross as a baptismal token; a baptismal prayer or hymn or psalm together with the scattering of water, at the outset of the service; the confession of the baptismal creed in the course of the service; or intercessions for those who are coming to be baptized. Furthermore, Christians do a whole series of things as part of the Sunday assembly that belong essentially to what it means to be baptized: participation in intercessions for the sake of the world; sharing the peace with each other; engaging in ministries of service in the assembly; coming to communion; being sent in witness and service in the world; remembering the poor. The basic garment that many Christians, lay and ordained, put on when they help to lead the service is the garment of baptism. This white alb is worn on behalf of the whole assembly. Baptism is the foundation of what we do here, this garment proclaims. Baptism belongs to every Sunday.

Thus, Justin, our second-century lay theologian, had just concluded writing in his *Apology* about how Christians enact baptism, when he began his description of the Sunday meeting in this way:

> And for the rest after these things [after baptism is enacted] we continually remind each other of these things [of baptism]. Those who have the means help all those who are in want, and we continually meet together. And over all that we take to eat we bless the creator of all things through God's Son Jesus Christ and through the Holy Spirit. And on the day named after the sun all, whether they live in the city or the countryside, are gathered together in unity. . . . (*1 Apology* 67; for the full text of Justin's description, see pp. 79–80)

Note that, for Justin, helping the poor, meeting together as Christians, and giving thanks over food all seem to be ways that the baptized remind each other of baptism. By this understanding, the Sunday meeting itself, which is the primary instance of all of these things—of meeting together, giving trinitarian thanks over the central gift of common food in the eucharist, and collecting food and money for the wretched and hungry in the city—is a reminder of baptism.

In recent times, we have come to see that frequent remembrance of baptism is important for us all to understand what the church most truly is. Good pastoral practice urges us to set a strong remembrance of baptism and a gracious clarity about the way one comes to baptism in every Christian gathering, in order to invite and welcome the puzzled newcomer, to have available the deepest possible response to the newcomer's inquiry about God and grace. Not uncommonly now, people come to church and find a basin or pool of water near the door, welcoming them. Furthermore, the increasingly widespread ecumenical practice discourages baptizing people in private, in purely family rites, as a contradiction of the very meaning of baptism. The washing will best take place in the parish community. Even in cases of emergency, more and more churches try to assemble as many people from the community as possible to assist with the washing. Current liturgical practice urges us to consider using the great festivals of the year—Easter, especially, but also Epiphany and Pentecost and All Saints—as primary times for baptizing, thereby making the return of those festivals each year into a return of baptismal meaning. Pastors sometimes take troubled individuals to a baptismal font to speak to them of the mercy of God, reminding them of their baptism. Even our funerals hold something of the water: the body set near the font or under the great garment of baptism (the pall) or near the great candle, and baptismal texts spoken or sung as grounds for the promise of life in the midst of death.

But the principal remembrance of baptism is in the Sunday gathering, week after week. Besides the gathering itself, its thanksgiving over food, and its collection for the poor—Justin's ways of remembrance— Lutheran Christians especially use confession and forgiveness as a "creeping back to baptism" at the beginning of the Sunday service. In the Reformation, confession and forgiveness were sometimes together called "repentance" (Latin: *poenitentia*; German: *Busse*). Speaking of that repentance, Luther once wrote these remarkable lines:

> Therefore baptism remains forever. Even though someone falls from it and sins, we always have access to it so that we may again subdue the old creature. But we need not have the water poured over us again. Even if we were immersed in water a hundred times, it would nevertheless not be more than one baptism, and the effect and significance would continue and remain. Repentance, therefore, is nothing else than a return and approach

to baptism, to resume and practice what has earlier been begun but abandoned.... Thus we see what a great and excellent thing baptism is, which snatches us from the jaws of the devil and makes us God's own, overcomes and takes away sin and daily strengthens the new person, and always endures and remains until we pass out of this misery into eternal glory. Therefore, let all Christians regard their baptism as the daily garment that they are to wear all the time. (*Large Catechism 4:77-79, 83-84*, in Kolb and Wengert, *The Book of Concord*, p. 466)

Then, what is this bath, that it should be so central? Isn't it simply the way we start someone out on the Christian life? Yes, but it is far more than that. Or, rather, in our beginning, when that beginning is made by God, is already hidden all the realities of our middle and our end, of our full life, of our death and of our life in God. In our beginning is not just our *selves*, but ourselves held in Christ's hands together with all those who belong to Christ, with all the church. In Christ, before God, by the Spirit, we are essentially *an assembly*. It is that assembly, that baptismal reality, that comes to expression week after week in the Sunday gathering. We need to see these things more clearly in the ways we celebrate baptism. The church is to make a great deal of this beginning—for every child and for every adult coming fresh to the community—and each member of the church is to come again and again to this beginning as a way to get through every day with faith.

Baptism is a washing with water in the name and by the command of Jesus Christ, such that the one who is washed is joined to Christ, under the Spirit of God, before the face and voice of God, in the company of all the church. Every baptism participates in the meaning of the stories of the baptism of Jesus himself (Mark 1:9-11 and parallels): the candidate goes into the water with Christ, the Spirit descends, and the voice of the Father calls this one a beloved child. Such is baptism "in the name of the Father and of the Son and of the Holy Spirit" (Matt. 28:19). Baptism is an immersion—even *burial*—in water and a rising to new life. Every baptism participates in the meaning of the stories of the death and resurrection of Christ, his final "baptism" (Mark 10:38; Luke 12:50): "Do you not know that all of us who have been baptized into Christ Jesus were baptized into his death? Therefore we have been buried with him by baptism into death, so that, just as Christ was raised from the dead by the glory of the Father, so we too might walk in newness of life" (Rom. 6:3-4). Because of these things, using the biblical-poetic language of the church, we may say that every baptism is God hovering over the water, creating the world anew; Noah and the people with Noah and all the animals surviving the flood; the people coming across the sea to freedom; water springing from the rock in the desert; the world renewed with living water; the womb of the church giving birth.

Washing with water in order to be ready for God already existed in the time of Jesus' ministry. In various ways, religious washings were part of the movements for renewal that marked the Judaism of the time of Christian origins, movements we know best by the New Testament evidence of John the Baptist's baptisms. Just as with the reading of scriptures in a communal assembly and the eating of a meal as a prayer, this washing was also taken by Jesus and his followers to be done in a new way as a means for proclaiming the grace of God. Only now, Christians were not to wash repeatedly, hoping to be pure for God's coming. Nor did they do the ritual washing for themselves alone. They were washed in Jesus' name, into the reality of God as God was encountered in Jesus Christ. They were washed together, into an assembly. And they were washed once, thereby joining the community that believed the hoped-for day of God's coming had already begun, in Jesus' death and in his resurrection. God had brought them into that dawning day, once-and-for-all, through the water.

It is this washing that we still do. Paradoxically, we have sometimes let the practice of the washing "shrink" into a smaller deed of less and less consequence. Some have seen baptism as essentially a thing done to babies, a passage rite at birth to launch the child into life. Others have regarded it as an optional symbol, useful to express one's own decision for faith. But the deep human longing for God to come openly, for justice to occur, for tears to be wiped away and deep thirsts to be slaked, for the world to be covered with the knowledge of God as waters cover the sea, is still alive in us. The recovery of a vigorous baptismal practice is about this ancient longing. The water-washing and the teaching that leads to the water-washing and the constant remembrance of the water-washing all mean to say: God is with us. God comes into the most God-forsaken places, the places summed up in Jesus' cross. The wiping away of tears has begun in the resurrection, and that beginning is washed over us in baptism. God's grace for the world is washed over us, and we are made a witness of the coming.

As with word and table, "bath" is also made up of two things. There is the water and there is the name. Christian baptism is made up of *water*, as much water as possible, poured over the candidate as a washing, as a drowning, as a birthing, as a gift of life and grace. At the same time, Christian baptism is the *teaching* about God, about God's grace, about God known in Jesus, about the mercy of the Holy Trinity. That teaching is the "name" of God, God's own self and power encountered and called upon. Such teaching leads to the font. It is discussed between candidates and sponsors and teachers on the way to the font. It is summed up in the name of God confessed at the font, the word proclaimed at the font. It is gathered up in the "catechism," the things learned in the baptismal process: the commandments, the creed, the prayer of Jesus, the words spoken in the sacraments, the way of return to baptism through absolution. This teaching is returned to throughout life.

The two things of baptism—the name and the bath, side-by-side, or the water and the teaching—also press us toward a third: toward community with each other. That is, water and the name bring us toward reminding each other of these things, toward communally bearing witness to the grace of God in the world. Baptism brings us to the assembly.

Every time the assembly gathers, we are back together in the gift and calling of baptism. We are once again constituted as the body of Christ. In fact, when the church gathers, there is in the gathering place no more important sign of Christ than the assembly of people itself. That assembly—and each of its members, including especially the least of them—needs to be honored and loved by those who serve it.

And because of that assembly, both the font and the name need to be "unshrunk" in our practice. The name in which we baptize needs to be much more than a formula or a ritual confession of faith. Our churches will do well to recover a process of teaching and formation that leads to baptism and flows from baptism for both adult and infant candidates. We need sponsors, mentors or godparents, cate- chists or teachers, pastors and members of the local community who take with great seriousness their roles in accompanying those who are being baptized. We need to help each other be less afraid to speak about God and grace to those who have begun to be curious about the hope that is in us. Then we need to let the washing itself be a powerful event, mirroring in the force of its symbol and ritual at least a little of the huge consequence of its meaning. We need to make our pools larger, when we can. We need to keep water in our fonts or pools all of the time. We need actually to wash or immerse our candidates, loving them, helping them across the water. We need to clothe them, anoint them, give them burning lights, sign them with the cross, lead them into the assembly, give them the holy food to eat and drink, talk with them of what happened to them, think with them of what we shall do together now to bear witness to God's mercy in the world.

Of course, there are disagreements among Christians about bap- tism, too. Shall we only baptize believers or are the infant children brought by believers to be candidates as well? Must the washing include a full submersion or is pouring or even sprinkling enough? Once again, even these disagreements ought not distract us from the astonishing gift, the sign of God's new age, that we have been given in common.

In fact, the disagreement about "believers' baptism" can push us all deeper, toward renewal. The ecumenical statement on *Baptism, Eucharist and Ministry* proposes:

> In order to overcome their differences, believer baptists and those who practice infant baptism should reconsider certain aspects of their practices. The first may seek to express more visibly the fact that children are placed under the protection of God's grace. The latter must guard themselves against the practice of apparently indiscriminate baptism and take more seriously their responsibility for the nurture of baptized children to mature commitment to Christ. (Baptism, 16, p. 6)

Thus, the tasks for believer baptizing groups are seeing that grace is indeed operative in baptism and regarding the children of believers as, in some sense, enrolled candidates for baptism, the washing itself to be enacted as they grow in years. The tasks for infant baptizers involve welcoming a serious process for teaching and forming the baptized in discipleship and faith. For both, unshrinking the name will help.

So will unshrinking the font, though if we are tempted to argue with each other about how much water we use, we may be helped by reading the wonderful first- or second-century text of the *Didache*:

> Concerning baptism, baptize thus: Having first rehearsed all these things [the nascent catechism], "baptize, in the Name of the Father and of the Son and of the Holy Spirit," in running water; but if thou hast no running water, baptize in other water, and if thou canst not in cold, then in warm. But if thou hast neither, pour water three times on the head. . . . (7:1-3, in *The Apostolic Fathers*, pp. 319–321)

As much water as possible is ideal. But there is no requirement, there is only grace. Water and the name are what are essential to Christian worship. Yet that is no excuse for minimalism, as if God would be pleased if we did less, spoke less, used less. It is *we* who need the washing of the water and the teaching of the name in stronger forms.

And it is we who need the assembly. *Assembly*—that word has been used repeatedly here. Again, the word *worship* could mislead us into thinking that we are talking about ways that Christians may privately praise God and that the gathering of Christians is simply a collection of those private ways in one room. In fact, the classic Christian approach to worship has gone in just the other direction. I need the community in order to hear that word of grace and life—on the lips of my sister or brother and of all those gathered—that word I cannot make up for myself or speak to myself. I need the assembly to be baptized and to remind me of my baptism. I need the community to celebrate the supper.

By the mercy of God, when we come to the central things, we are given all of these things, together.

For reflection and discussion

1. What do you think is the "name of God"? Why?
2. How is baptism, as practiced in your congregation, like the baptism of Jesus? How is it like Jesus' death and resurrection?
3. Who wears what liturgical vestments in your assembly? Why?
4. Have you been a baptismal sponsor? What does that role mean to you? Does it continue to be important in your life?
5. In what ways is baptism remembered in your Sunday assembly?
6. How might the water and the name be "unshrunk" in your congregation?
7. Is there water near the door of your Sunday gathering? What does its location mean to you?

7
Style, Ceremony, and Purpose in Doing the Central Things

So these are the essentials of Christian worship: An *assembly* gathers in *prayer* around the *scriptures read* and *preached*, both reading and preaching taking place so that Christ is encountered as the mercy of God and the source of life. This community of the word then tastes the meaning of that word by keeping the meal of Christ, *giving thanks* over bread and cup and *eating and drinking*. It is this word-table community, this "body of Christ" enlivened by the Spirit and standing before God, that gathers other people to its number, continually *teaching* both itself and these newcomers the mercy and mystery of God and *washing* them in the name of that God. This teaching and washing, this word and water together—this "baptism"—constitute the foundation of the assembly, the source of its vocation and life, to which it continually returns. All of these essential things urge the community toward the world, toward prayer for the world, sharing with the hungry of the world, caring for the world, giving witness to the world, and loving the others of the world. All of these essential things, together, proclaim and give the mercy of God in Christ. Such is *worship in word and sacrament*. Such are the central things we hold and that we discover to be holding us. The bell rings out an invitation to this worship:

> To the bath and the table,
> To the prayer and the word,
> I call every seeking soul.

Around these central things, which will be most evident in Sunday and festival worship, other gatherings of Christians may also take place. Like planets around the sun, these other gatherings reflect the light of the central Sunday gathering. They do so mostly by repeating and echoing the baptismal identity, the psalms, the readings, the songs, the prayers, and the blessings of the Sunday assembly, using these echoes to mark sunrise, work, sunset, and rest in every day, using them to go out into the occasions of life. Some of these other gatherings help inquirers, newcomers, and candidates for baptism to come more deeply into the mystery at the heart of the Sunday assembly, reading and discussing the scriptures with them, rehearsing the preaching, praying for them. Both sorts of Christian gatherings—daily prayer and catechumenal gatherings—come to their purpose most clearly as they depend upon the full Christian assembly around the central things.

Certain dangers arise in talking about this short list of the essentials of Christian worship. For one thing, people may forget what the central things are for, why they are essential. A church may begin to think that simply to read the scripture and hear a sermon is enough, for whatever purpose they are done: ideological training, denominational aggrandizement, self-realization, the acquisition of power, the attempt to please God. Or a community may begin to do the eucharist, to give formal thanks and do the eating and drinking for a variety of skewed reasons: to ensure a good crop, to win a war, to sanctify a government, to heighten the solidarity of a particular racial or sexual or economic group, to win a football game, to help the dead get to heaven. Or the washing and naming of God may take place simply to mark a birth, as a particular culture's rite of passage. Or any one of these things may be forced on people, in ways utterly devoid of the love to which the central things themselves bear witness.

No. The reasons for these essential things belong to their essential character. Word, table, bath, and prayers occur at the heart of a participating assembly so that all people may freely encounter God's mercy in Christ, that they may come to faith again and again, that they may be formed into a community of faith, that they may stand in dignity, life, and freedom before God, that they may be brought to the possibility of love for God's world, that they may become part of God's own mission of love toward the world. When these purposes are not manifest in the exercise of the central things themselves, the deep meaning of the central things is obscured and betrayed. Even so, God acts in these things. God's life-giving Spirit breaks out of our prisons. Even where the scripture reading is turned to oppressive ends, the meal celebrated for manipulative religious purpose, or the meaning of baptism forgotten, the combination of the liberating words of scripture with the gracious actions given by Christ can yield faith. Where we have most smothered and misused the holy things, fire can still leap out into the hearts and lives of the assembly.

But our business is to see that the celebration of these central things accords with their meaning, not for God's sake but for ours.

The other great danger of speaking about the essentials of Christian worship is that we take such speech as minimalist counsel: do only such things as barely count to meet the "essential" requirements. No. The word *essential* here is intended to mean just the opposite. Let these things be central. Let them stand at the center, large and full, influencing and determining all else we do. Let these things themselves be larger. Let the scripture reading be done as if it were clearly the first reason we have come together at all; let it be done as if it were the very Book of Life. Let the preaching be more serious, more profound, more gracious than we have recently experienced. Let the prayers be truly intercessions, the real naming of the needs of the world before God. Let the meal be held every Sunday. Let the food be clearly food. Let the hungry be always remembered. Let the thanksgiving be beautiful and strong. Let the whole assembly eat and drink. Let both the font and the name be "unshrunk."

There remain, of course, a hundred open questions. With what music shall we do these things? With what leadership? Shall the style of our assembly be informal or formal or something in between? Shall we hold books in our hands, so that a rich variety of written texts and complex music can be employed by all the people? Or shall the words be simple, known by heart, and the music a refrain or call-and-response, with a choir leading us? How shall these central things be enacted so that they are seen to be hospitable to a diversity of cultures? What shall be the spatial configuration of our assembly? How, exactly, will we gather around the word, the table, and the water pool? Shall our gathering together, our entry, be slow and intentional or direct and to the point? How long will the meeting of our assembly take?

The very centrality of bath, word, prayer, table, and the assembly around them—and the reasons for their centrality—while not determining absolute answers to these and many other questions, do begin to give us some characteristics of the mode of our celebration. These characteristics, while not exactly essentials of Christian worship, are corollaries that ought not be easily ignored. A list of such characteristics should include architectural and ritual focus, a music that serves, the importance of Sunday and other festivals, an assembly that actually participates, many ministries, and a recognized presider who is in communion with the churches.

In classical Reformation theology, most of these characteristics are considered to belong to the *adiaphora*, the things that are indifferent, the things that are *not* essential. Our relationship with God rests on none of these things. Still, one should be careful with *adiaphora*. It is not that one can do whatever one likes with these matters, even leaving them out altogether. There will be secondary matters in any Christian service. Rather, one must ask how those secondary matters are arranged, so as to disclose and assist the things that are primary.

For instance, many kinds of buildings or even outdoor arrangements may serve for the Christian assembly. Our building does not bring us to God or show us Christ or force the Spirit's coming. But it follows from the centrality of the essential things that the building or outdoor arrangement will need to be one that can be hospitable to all the people who come and can immediately draw them toward the word, the prayers, the table, and the font. Architectural clichés for holiness—say, buildings filled with great religious art intended for personal contemplation or classic temples, buildings for a god or for a priesthood approaching a god—will serve poorly for this purpose. Architecture with an originally domestic or secular public purpose will probably be more easily adapted to the purposes of the Christian assembly. But even there, the domestic will need to be broken open to include many more people than are usual for homes and to include a wide-open, public door. And a public building will need to focus on a book, a table, a water pool, and people welcome in love to come to them, not on a judge or a performing artist or a dramatic stage. Even an outdoor space will need to be carefully arranged. Such a space can show the simplicity and focus of the Christian meeting. It also can provide the opportunity to be distracted, not gathered together and paying attention to each other and the central things at all. The task of building a room or shaping a space for the church is, in every culture, a difficult and wonderful challenge.

Similarly, many kinds of songs or ritual may make up the flow of the service. But it will need to be clear that the flow of the meeting is into and out of the central things. A choir anthem or a drama that does not serve the assembly's gathering in the word—one that turns what was a participating assembly into an audience, alienating them from their own event—is as great a problem now as it was in the Middle Ages. We will need to keep asking about style and music, about how we gather and how we proceed, but these questions always need to be balanced with an inquiry about whether our answers are helping people to do the central things or are distracting them and turning them aside. Amplification, for example, may so magnify the voice of the presider or of the music group that it dwarfs or even silences the voice of the assembly. On the other hand, amplification—when it is well-done—can serve the assembly magnificently and inconspicuously as it gathers around the word. Similarly, a great video or projection screen filled with images of the leader or of projected words, even when they are being used out of a desire to help, can make it almost impossible to see the book, the living, human-sized reader or preacher, or the font with its water, or the table with its bread and cup, at the center of the meeting. On the other hand, beautifully crafted projection might be like the wall-painting or the stained-glass windows of the current time, if it is indeed crafted to support—rather than to distract from—word, prayers, bath, table, and assembly.

Music itself is a further and most important case in point. Many sorts of music can and have served the Christian community. This creative development should continue. But music that exalts the performer and silences the community, music that has no room for the whole assembly's voice, music that is marked only by despair or only by happiness, music about "me," music turned in on itself will have much difficulty serving the gathering around the central things. Indeed, that whole gathering, at its best, is musical in its variety of voices, its timing, its silences, its rhythms and resolutions. The Lutheran churches have, since their earliest days, used both hymns and chant—at least two kinds of music—to unfold the flow of the whole service. Lutheran people have echoed that assembly flow by singing the same hymns at home and by learning the chants by heart. Today, in every Christian community, it will be good if the musical character of the assembly is always coming to expression in actual music, new and old, in several kinds. But this music will have to *serve*, taking its power to evoke and to gather and turning this power toward the needs of the people as they sing around word and prayers, bath and table. Such music will let the primary role of the choir be to lead this people. The creation of a liturgical music—a pastoral music—is also a difficult and wonderful challenge in every era and every culture.

One might say it this way: hundreds of people may flock to a Christian church because of its impressive architecture, its grand organ, its Baroque music program, its gospel choir, its band, its inspirational preaching, its programs of self-help, or its use of multimedia or innovative dance. These things may, as Luther would say, "show forth Christ," but they also may not. The popularity of these things cannot be the measuring stick. Their service to the central, essential things can.

Even though we have not listed Sunday or certain festivals among the essentials of Christian worship, it should be clear that Sunday matters a great deal to Christians. So does Easter and the cycle of days that lead to and from Easter. Sunday and Easter ought not be set aside unless for serious reason. Because the essential things of Christian worship are those things that, by the Spirit's gift and Christ's promise, gather us into the identity of Christ before the face of God, it is clear why Sunday and the principal festivals matter. They are about the identity of Christ. Every Sunday proclaims that the God who made the world has raised Jesus up. Sunday, then, is properly the day for assembly around the very things—bath, word, and table—which regularly show this resurrection to us. Easter is a kind of Sunday to the year. Indeed, the great Three Days that lead to and include the nighttime Easter Vigil especially focus around all the central things. Christians can and do gather on other days. All days are holy; none are closer to God. But as long as the gospels are read, Sunday will have priority as the day of Christian assembly and Easter will be the most important of the annual observances of the Christian community.

Assembly itself is not adiaphoral in Christian worship. It may sometimes, of necessity, be a small assembly: the gathering of Christians in the room of someone sick or dying, for example. But we cannot do without it. The central things belong essentially in the open, public assembly of Christians. Then my private prayer recalls these things, turns them over in my heart, rehearses them, repeats them before God: "These things I remember, as I pour out my soul: how I went with the throng and led them in procession to the house of God" (Ps. 42:4).

But such a gathering is not a collective, not a crowd, not a mob, not a cheering section, not a club, not a marketing niche. In a Christian gathering, each person should be welcomed, each person respected for his or her baptismal dignity or for the mystery God made in that individual and Christ redeemed. Each person's gifts are to be brought in ways that serve the assembly's purpose. Each person is to be cared for and honored, in the distribution of the holy supper for example, with love. There should be space, hospitality, respect, silence, room for one's own thoughts, no compulsion, no forcing of people to recite texts they have never seen and do not believe. This is a *personal* communal gathering.

And it is a participating assembly. By the songs and actions that surround the central things it should be evident that *we* gather for the word, *we* enact the bath, *we* hold the supper. When it is at all possible, congregations should hold just one Sunday gathering for word and sacrament, to avoid the marketing temptations of our culture and to make clear how important this communal "we" is, how we are "the body of Christ," not a group that happens to like a certain kind of music. This participation comes to focused expression when from the baptized people assembled here, various people are drawn to minister in love to the assembly: greeters, ushers, musicians, cantors, and the rehearsed voices of the choir, readers of scripture, a leader of the intercessions, bringers of gifts, ministers of communion and those chosen to bear the bread and cup away to the absent, catechists, sponsors. The repeated juxtapositions of two things that make up the essence of Christian worship—scripture readings next to preaching, thanksgiving next to passing out the food, teaching next to the bath, word next to sacrament—will be more clearly manifest if different persons are heard reading the scripture, giving out the food, helping with the teaching. Called "assisting ministers" in current Lutheran sources, these lay persons assist the assembly to do its central liturgical work. Certainly, we can do the central things without these offices being filled, with only one ordained leader, for example. But the fuller expression of the central things, a celebration that accords with their meaning, calls for these ministries. And we cannot do without a participating assembly.

Neither can we do without a presider. Some churches regard a presider who is ordained (that is, one who has been publicly prayed for and is regarded as being in communion with the church) as one of the essentials of Christian worship. Other churches take such leadership for granted, doing the ordinations, but hesitating to call this essential lest one demote the central word, table, and font this presider is called upon to serve. This is not the place for that debate. It can only be asserted here that the agreement is greater than is ordinarily seen. When the ministry of the presider is placed where it belongs—within the participating assembly gathered around the central things—there is an astonishing concurrence on the need for such a leader: to speak the lively word in response to the readings or to see that such a word is spoken; to pray at table; to see to it that there is a collection for the poor; and to preside amidst the process that leads to and through the water. The ministry of the presider is abused and misformed if, rather than serve the people around these central things, it calls attention to itself, to the importance and personality of the minister. Widespread agreement is also found about the need for such a local leader to be in a wider communion, to be one of the local symbols of this community's connection to all the other churches. A disagreement between Christians remains—a disagreement we need to continue to work on as we labor together for the manifestation of Christian unity—about the nature and meaning of this wider connection.

These assertions about the nature of Christian worship generally do not mean to deny the distinctions among Lutheran worship or Anglican worship or Roman Catholic worship or Methodist worship.

Lutheran liturgy, for example, treasures hymnody as a nearly essential part of its gatherings, and Lutherans will often repeat the paradox that while *we* do all the good things of the liturgy, it is finally *God* who is the actor. Methodist worship shares the interest in hymnody and has sometimes rephrased the list of the "means of grace" to include things such as "searching the scripture." Roman Catholic worship treasures the patterns of the ancient church of the city of Rome as paradigmatic, always seeking to translate those patterns into new situations and new languages. Furthermore, local churches of one country, belonging to one jurisdiction, rightly try to order their own liturgical life using more than simply the "essentials," publishing books and seeking a unity, in both essentials and nonessentials, that will enable them to carry on a common life marked by mutual recognition. American Episcopalians from different areas and cultural backgrounds share many of the same words and gestures, having a single *Book of Common Prayer*. Many American Lutherans share a significant amount of common music. This is, on the whole, a good thing.

But these differences are less great than we usually think. Or when they are great, we need to ask ourselves if they are obscuring the central things. Lutheran worship at its deepest—and this is true of all Western and Eastern Christian worship, as well—is this: a participating and open assembly, served by its ministers, gathered around the bath, the word, the prayers, the table—the very matters which speak and sign Jesus Christ so that the nations may live.

It is these essential things that we all need.

Bath, table, prayer, word, and an assembly of seeking souls—there is our simple list. Or, put in action, we gather through the water; we hear the scriptures read and preached and we pray; we set a table, give thanks, eat and drink, and send to the poor. We do the whole thing musically. We work to keep the door open, for going out as well as for coming in. And, most deeply, we realize that God has been the actor here, and then we are sent ourselves.

These things are the central things, the marks of worship in word and sacrament.

But, once again, why?

Because they are the gift of God for the life of the world, and because by them God continually brings us again, together, into faith and so into hope and love.

For reflection and discussion

1. What is your favorite hymn? If that hymn were to be so placed in the service that it would serve the flow of the event—support the central things—where would you place it?

2. Have you participated in an Easter Vigil? How does its outline of Light, Word, Bath, and Table especially focus us on all the central things?

3. Does your congregation have more than one service on Sunday? Why? Is it a good idea or not?

4. What gifts should lay people have before they are chosen to be assisting ministers, readers, leaders of prayer, servers of communion? What skills should they work on training as they prepare to do this ministry?

5. What gifts should pastors have in order to preside? What skills should they work on training in order to preside?

6. What is the focus of the room where your congregation meets, your "sanctuary"? If you could, how would you remodel or rearrange the room?

7. If you are a Lutheran, what would you say are the characteristics of Lutheran worship? If you belong to another confession or denomination, how would you characterize the worship of that group?

8. What would have been your grandparents' ideas about what is central in worship? How would those ideas be the same or different from what is written in this book? How would it be the same or different from your own ideas?

Justin Martyr's Description of the Sunday Meeting

1 Apology 67

And for the rest after these things [after baptism is enacted] we continually remind each other of these things [of baptism]. Those who have the means help all those who are in want, and we continually meet together. And over all that we take to eat we bless the creator of all things through God's Son Jesus Christ and through the Holy Spirit. And on the day named after the sun all, whether they live in the city or the countryside, are gathered together in unity. Then the records of the apostles or the writings of the prophets are read for as long as there is time. When the reader has concluded, the presider in a discourse admonishes and invites us into the pattern of these good things. Then we all stand together and offer prayer. And, as we said before, when we have concluded the prayer, bread is set out to eat, together with wine and water. The presider likewise offers up prayer and thanksgiving, as much as he can, and the people sing out their assent saying the *amen*. There is a distribution of the things over which thanks have been said and each person participates, and these things are sent by the deacons to those who are not present. Those who are prosperous and who desire to do so, give what they wish, according to each one's choice, and the collection is deposited with the presider. He aids orphans and widows, those who are in want through disease or through another cause, those who are in prison, and foreigners who are sojourning here. In short, the presider is a guardian to all those who are in need. We hold this meeting together on the day of the sun since it is the first day, on which day God, having transformed darkness and matter, made the world. On the same day Jesus Christ our savior rose from the dead . . . he appeared to his apostles and disciples and taught them these things which we have presented also to you for your consideration.

For this translation and further comment, see Gordon W. Lathrop, Holy Things: A Liturgical Theology *(Minneapolis: Fortress, 1993), 45, and* Holy Ground: A Liturgical Cosmology *(Minneapolis: Fortress, 2003), 137–138.*

For Further Reading

Baptism, Eucharist and Ministry. Faith and Order Paper 111. Geneva: World Council of Churches, 1982. The basic ecumenical document about the centrality of baptism and holy communion in the life of the churches. It should be read in conjunction with the Ditchingham Report, *Towards Koinonia in Worship*, found in the volume *So We Believe, So We Pray* mentioned next.

Best, Thomas F., and Dagmar Heller, eds. *So We Believe, So We Pray: Towards Koinonia in Worship*, Faith and Order Paper 171. Geneva: World Council of Churches, 1995. Papers from the 1994 Ditchingham Consultation on the relationship between Christian worship and Christian unity. The Ditchingham Report, found here, is also partly reprinted in Gordon W. Lathrop, *Holy People: A Liturgical Ecclesiology* (Minneapolis: Fortress, 1999), 229–232.

Gaillardetz, Richard R. *Transforming Our Days: Spirituality, Community and Liturgy in a Technological Culture*. New York: Crossroad, 2000. A fascinating study by a lay Roman Catholic theologian about how the matters called "central things" here are to be considered "focal practices," casting a renewing light on ordinary daily life.

Koenker, Ernest. *Worship in Word and Sacrament.* St. Louis: Concordia, 1959. A small classic of Lutheran thought, still important and readable, if a little dated in language.

Lange, Dirk G., ed. *Bath, Word, Prayer and Table: A Liturgical Primer.* Akron: Order of St. Luke, 2005. A fresh and readable ecumenical introduction to Christian worship, organized around the central things but written from a wide variety of viewpoints.

Lathrop, Gordon W., and Timothy J. Wengert. *Christian Assembly: Marks of the Church in a Pluralistic Age.* Minneapolis: Fortress, 2004. An unfolding of the historical origin and practical significance of the Lutheran proposal to all the churches: Word and sacraments are the marks of the church.

Principles for Worship, Renewing Worship, vol. 2. Minneapolis: Augsburg Fortress, 2002. Besides profound and accessible statements on worship language, music, preaching, and worship space, includes the important text, *The Use of the Means of Grace.*

Ramshaw, Gail. *A Three-Year Banquet: The Lectionary for the Assembly.* Minneapolis: Augsburg Fortress, 2004. The best introduction to the meaning and practice of the ecumenical three-year lectionary currently available.

———. *Sunday Morning.* Chicago: Liturgy Training Publications, 1993. A picture book for children and their parents and for us all about the shape and meaning of Sunday worship.

———. *The Three-Day Feast: Maundy Thursday, Good Friday, Easter.* Minneapolis: Augsburg Fortress, 2004. Helps to locate the central things at the heart of the Christian year.

———. *Under the Tree of Life: The Religion of a Feminist Christian.* Akron: Order of St. Luke, 2003. "Each Sunday morning," the Lutheran author writes, "we savor the water, the bread, the wine. . . . So we practice the faith" (page vi).

Schmemann, Alexander. *For the Life of the World.* New York: St. Vladimir's Seminary Press, 1973. An Eastern Orthodox reflection, intended originally for an ecumenical gathering of college students, about the urgent importance of the central things.

Schattauer, Thomas H., ed. *Inside Out: Worship in an Age of Mission.* Minneapolis: Fortress, 1999. A collection of essays by Lutheran teachers of worship. Especially the essay of the editor himself, "Liturgical Assembly as a Locus of Mission," gives support to the understanding of the central things as places where God acts in mission for the life of the world.

Stauffer, S. Anita, ed. *Worship and Culture in Dialogue* (1994), *Christian Worship: Unity in Cultural Diversity* (1996), and *Baptism, Rites of Passage and Culture* (1999). Geneva: Lutheran World Federation. Reports of a series of consultations held by the Lutheran World Federation together with ecumenical participation. Much of the work of these consultations, including the important Nairobi Statement found in the 1996 volume, consider the ways word and sacrament ought to be celebrated in diverse cultural contexts throughout the world.

Torvend, Samuel. *Daily Bread, Holy Meal: Opening the Gifts of Holy Communion.* Minneapolis: Augsburg Fortress, 2004. The best small book about the meaning of the Lord's supper currently available.

Willimon, William H. *Word, Water, Wine and Bread: How Worship Has Changed over the Years.* Valley Forge: Judson, 1980. A simple, accessible account of the history of Christian worship, written by a Methodist pastor and theologian.

OTHER Worship Matters TITLES

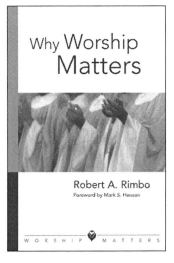

Why Worship Matters
by Robert A. Rimbo
Foreword by
Mark S. Hanson

Why Worship Matters is the first volume in a series centering on the Renewing Worship project of the Evangelical Lutheran Church in America. This little volume is a conversation-starter for those who want to look at the assembly's worship in very broad terms. It also invites reflection on the needs of the world, individuals, the church, and society in light of the assembly's central activity, worshiping God.

08066-5108-3

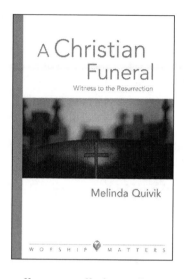

A Christian Funeral: Witness to the Resurrection

by Melinda Quivik

It is one thing to simply bury the dead. It is another to participate in a liturgy that celebrates with honesty the life that has ended, engages the pain of the loss, and proclaims the Christian hope in the resurrection. Because we don't talk very well about the questions raised by death—either in our culture or in our churches—this book invites you to learn some of the history and theology surrounding concepts of the afterlife so that you will be better equipped to plan a funeral that is not simply a utilitarian exercise but a vital and essential font of faith.

0-8066-5148-2

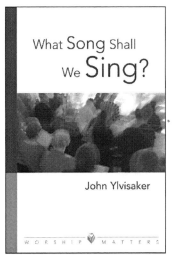

What Song Shall We Sing?

by John Ylvisaker

Much has been written about worship wars and the perceived need for recognizing and implementing different styles of music in the service, whether it be quiet, unaccompanied singing at the one extreme or bands powered by electric guitars and synths at the other. Less has been written about fusing musical styles. This book explores the way hymns are put together and how the fusion technique can heal the wounds of the worship wars. A look at the changing role of vocal and instrumental leadership becomes part of the discussion, with the goal being to bring people together through music.

0-8066-5149-0

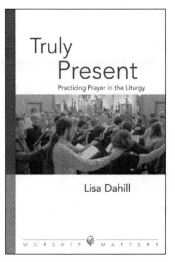

Truly Present: Practicing Prayer in the Liturgy
by Lisa Dahill

Humans hunger for contemplative prayer. In this readable and practical volume Dahill discusses the need for rediscovering such prayer forms in the ELCA, and introduces Lutheran liturgical spirituality very broadly. Each chapter is devoted to one prayer practice grounded in the liturgy and shows how each contemplative practice both roots within and in turn also deepens our experience of worship.

0-8066-5147-4

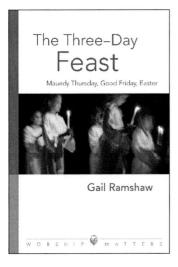

The Three-Day Feast: Maundy Thursday, Good Friday, Easter
by Gail Ramshaw

An introduction to the great Three Days in the church's year that celebrate Christ's passage from death to life. Using the motifs of "telling the story" and "enacting the meaning," Ramshaw illuminates the significance of each day's worship and makes plain the history, symbolism, meaning, and centrality of these core days of the church's life together.

0-8066-5115-6

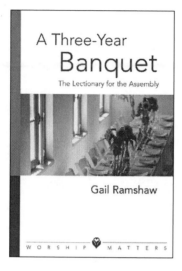

A Three-Year Banquet: The Lectionary for the Assembly
by Gail Ramshaw

A Three-Year Banquet invites the entire worshiping assembly, lay and clergy, to understand and delight in the three-year lectionary. The study guide explains how the Revised Common Lectionary was developed and how the gospels, the first readings, and the epistles are assigned. Further chapters describe many ways that the three readings affect the assembly's worship and the assembly itself. Like food at a banquet, the fare we enjoy in the lectionary nourishes us year after year.

0-8066-5105-9

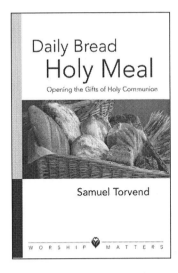

Daily Bread, Holy Meal: Opening the Gifts of Holy Communion
by Samuel Torvend

Daily Bread, Holy Meal invites Christians to reconsider the significance of eating and drinking with Jesus of Nazareth in a world of great need. Drawing on recent biblical and historical studies, this exploration of the Eucharist asks the seeker in every Christian to consider the ecological, theological, communal, and ethical dimensions of the Lord's supper. Through a careful weaving of biblical passages, medieval poetry, Luther's writings, familiar hymns, and newly-written liturgical texts, each chapter unfolds another "gift" of the Holy Communion and the sometimes troubling questions each one raises for individuals who live in a fast food culture yet seek community around a gracious table.

0-8066-5106-7

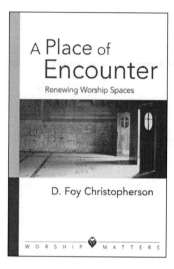

A Place of Encounter: Renewing Worship Spaces

by D. Foy Christopherson

House, temple, theatre, warehouse, courtroom, auditorium, TV studio, or lecture hall? River or baptistery or pool? Dining room or catacomb? House of God or house of the church? In its 2000-year history the church has tried on many buildings, and is ever seeking a more comfortable skin. Exactly what that skin will look like is guided by how the church understands itself, by how it worships, and by what it understands its mission to be. *A Place of Encounter* brings clarity and insight to congregations and individuals who are interested in exploring how our worship spaces serve, form, and proclaim.

0-8066-5107-5